CHANGING WOMAN AND HER SISTERS

CHANGING WOMAN

AND

HER SISTERS

Stories of Goddesses
from Around the World

Retold by

KATRIN HYMAN TCHANA

Illustrated by

TRINA SCHART HYMAN

HOLIDAY HOUSE / *New York*

Acknowledgments

Thank you to Barbara Ragas for your expert and merciless editing of this book and thank you, Michou, for listening patiently to these stories when they were unedited and had no pictures! Thank you, Xavier, for deciding to be born and slowing me down long enough to start writing. Thanks to Geneva Menge and Mrs. McCarthy and all the other volunteers at the Lyme Town Library for teaching me (and so many others) that I can always find out anything I need to know by going to the library, no matter how clueless I am. And thank you, Trina, for everything.

K. H. T.

The publisher would like to thank Shonto Begay for his expert reading of "Changing Woman."

Library of Congress Cataloging-in-Publication Data
Tchana, Katrin Hyman.
Changing Woman and her sisters: stories of goddesses from around the world /
by Katrin Hyman Tchana ; illustrated by Trina Schart Hyman.
p. cm.
Summary: An illustrated collection of traditional tales
which feature goddesses from different cultures, including Navajo,
Mayan, and Fon. Notes explain each goddess's place in her culture,
the reason for the book, and how the illustrations were developed.
Includes bibliographical references.
Contents: Changing Woman — Macha, goddess of horses —
Sedna, woman of the sea — Kuan Yin, the compassionate —
Isis, mistress of life and death — Ix Chel, the moon goddess —
Amaterasu, the sun goddess — Inanna, queen of heaven and earth —
Durga, the warrior goddess — Mawu, the creator.

ISBN-10: 0-8234-1999-1 (hardcover)
ISBN-13: 978-0-8234-1999-9 (hardcover)

1. Tales. 2. Goddesses—Folklore.
[1. Folklore. 2. Goddesses—Folklore.]
I. Hyman, Trina Schart, ill. II. Title.
PZ8.1.T19Cha 2006
[398.2]—dc22
2005052504

To Trina
K. H. T.

CONTENTS

CHANGING WOMAN
A NAVAJO DEITY

Central to the mythology of the Navajo people is Asdzaa Nadleii', Changing Woman. Sometimes she comes as a girl, other times as a young woman, or she may appear to be a middle-aged woman or an old grandmother. Changing Woman changes as the earth changes, young in spring and old in winter, but constantly renewed. In some stories she is considered to be the daughter of Earth Mother and Sky Father. Another story claims that she is the daughter of the two inner spirits of the earth: Long Life and Happiness. She is the mother of the Navajo hero twins, Monster Slayer and Born for Water. It is Changing Woman who created people and all the things that people need to keep them happy. Therefore, according to the Navajo tradition, we are all the children of Changing Woman.

Early one morning First Man was out walking. He saw a dark cloud had gathered on the top of the tallest mountain. He climbed the mountain and found a little baby girl lying on a circle of crystal sand. Rainbows danced over her head. Dawn and Darkness tossed the little baby between them, so that she cried and cried.

"What a beautiful baby she is!" cried First Man with delight. The baby's eyes were two perfect black ovals. Her body was white and clear, like a white shell. First Man laid the baby in a rainbow cradle and wrapped her up in a dark cloud. He laced the cloud with sun rays and took the baby home to First Woman.

"Oh, what a beautiful baby you've found!" First Woman crowed. She took the baby

in her arms and rocked her. As First Man and First Woman admired her, the baby began changing. First, she was a young woman of dazzling beauty. Next, she became a mature woman, handsome and strong. Then, she became a wrinkled old grandmother. In the blink of an eye, she turned back into a tiny baby again, kicking her little arms and beating her little legs against the sides of her rainbow cradle. My daughter, First Woman called her.

The baby grew and grew. In four days she could already talk and run around. She was a beautiful little girl. Changing Woman, First Man called her. And whenever the little girl heard the words *Changing Woman*, she came running.

The little girl grew and grew. In four days she was a big girl, strong and sturdy. Now she refused to eat the food that First Woman made for her. Every morning Dawn would send her magic pollen to eat, and in the evening Dusk also sent her magic pollen to eat. That was her food.

Changing Woman grew and grew, and in four more days she was a beautiful young maiden. The gods came and dressed her all in white. They gave her moccasins and leggings and a skirt made from white shell. They gave her a white shell headdress. They placed a perfect rock crystal in her mouth. They performed a ceremony in her honor and gave her the songs that are a blessing for all humankind.

"Go ahead and run, Changing Woman," said the gods encouraging her. So Changing Woman began to run, her white shells rattling with every bound. She ran to the east and the west, the north and the south. She circled all the mountains, and everywhere she ran, jewels sprang up under her feet. Even today there are precious stones on the mountains where Changing Woman ran.

Time passed and Changing Woman was fully grown. One day she climbed the mountain to bathe in a waterfall. As the cool water splashed down on her she watched the sun's rays make rainbows glitter on the foaming cascade. Suddenly a handsome man appeared. He seemed to walk right out of the ray of sunshine. He was the sun god. He smiled at Changing Woman, and Changing Woman felt her heart stop beating for an instant. Confused, she looked away. When she looked up again, the man was gone.

Changing Woman went home and told First Woman about the strange man she'd seen at the waterfall. First Woman scowled. "Don't go back there, my daughter," she warned her. "How many times must I tell you not to go wandering in the mountains by yourself? Don't you know that dangerous monsters are everywhere? The man you saw was probably a monster. Next time he might do more than simply smile at you. He might eat you right up!"

Changing Woman promised to be more careful. But the next day she felt strange movements inside her body. She asked First Woman about it. First Woman looked at her carefully. "I think you are going to have a baby!" First Woman declared.

Nine days later Changing Woman gave birth to two babies, twin boys. Their names were Monster Slayer and Born for Water. Changing Woman took good care of them. When she went to gather food, she hid them in a pit and covered it with a heavy stone. But when she came back, the babies had moved the stone and crawled out of the pit. They were rolling around on the ground, wrestling with each other.

In four days the babies had grown into big, strong boys. Their baby teeth fell out. Changing Woman made them new teeth out of white shell. First Man made bows and arrows for the boys. Now they ran everywhere, shooting at anything with their bows and arrows. But Changing Woman feared that monsters might catch them and harm them.

One day Monster Slayer, who was the older twin, asked his mother, "Who is our father?"

"You have no father," Changing Woman answered him.

Monster Slayer persisted. Four times he asked his mother the same question. Four times she gave him the same reply. When Monster Slayer asked a fifth time, Changing Woman told her sons the truth.

"My poor children," she said, "your father is the sun. But you mustn't try to visit him, for it's a very long and difficult journey to his house."

As usual, the twins had no thought for their own safety. They left their mother's house and traveled to the house of the sun. They had many adventures along the way and many adventures before they came back, but that is another story. They were gone for a long time.

When at last the twins returned home, Changing Woman did not recognize them. They wore armor made from flint and carried arrows of lightning. These were gifts from their father, the sun. With the lightning arrows they had killed many fierce monsters, but other monsters still lived.

"Mother, don't you recognize us?" the twins said, laughing. They took off their flint armor. Then Changing Woman saw that these were really her children, and she greeted them joyfully.

"And look, Mother," said Monster Slayer. "Our father has sent a gift to you." He presented her with five magical hoops: one black, one yellow, one blue, one white, and one that shone with all the colors of the rainbow.

Then Changing Woman took the black hoop and rolled it to the east. She rolled the blue hoop to the south, the yellow hoop to the west, and the white hoop to the north. She took the hoop of many colors and threw it straight up over her head. She blew a powerful breath on it, and it floated up into the sky and disappeared from view. As the hoops rolled away, thunder rumbled in the distance.

The sky grew dark, and a strong wind began to blow. Changing Woman looked around her and saw whirlwinds blowing in every direction. They uprooted trees as if they were weeds and tossed great rocks around as if they were little pebbles. Hailstones as large as a man's fist fell from the sky and pelted the earth below.

"My sons, I fear for our house," cried Changing Woman. "It is high in the mountains, and this wind will certainly destroy it."

Monster Slayer ran and covered the house with a black cloud. He tied the cloud down with rainbows and fastened a black fog all around it with sunbeams. For four days the gods huddled inside, listening to the storm that raged about them. On the morning of the fifth day, the winds died down and the sun rose in a pale blue sky. Everyone went outside to look around.

The storm had brought amazing changes to the earth. A giant canyon had formed by the side of the house. The shapes of the surrounding bluffs were different now. Pillars of rock rose up from the earth in strange towers.

"Surely all of the monsters are now dead," declared Changing Woman. "None could have survived this storm."

But a small wind came and whispered in their ears, "Old age still lives. Poverty still lives. Hunger still lives. The lice still live."

Monster Slayer sprang up. "I will go and kill them immediately," he cried.

But Changing Woman stopped him. "No, my son, leave them be. These monsters are bad, but they are also partly good. The humans who are soon coming to live on this earth must learn to use their courage and intelligence. These monsters will challenge them and help them grow."

So Monster Slayer let those monsters live, and they roam the earth to this day.

After the great storm that destroyed all the man-eating monsters and made the earth safe for human life, the gods returned to their own houses and went on with their work. Changing Woman continued to prepare the earth for the humans who were coming. She made horses and sheep, and wild animals for them to hunt. She created useful tools for them to cook and make clothing with. But soon she began to feel that there was no special reason to create any more things. Human beings were the only thing missing. She began to think she should go away to the west.

Soon all the gods knew that Changing Woman was going to live in the west. Nobody wanted Changing Woman to leave. But they knew there must be a reason for it.

One morning Changing Woman rose at dawn and called together the twelve gods and goddesses who would accompany her to her new home. They left within a dark cloud, surrounded by a dark mist. And when they had followed the path for a time that was neither short nor long, for it was not in our time, they arrived at the place where the earth meets the sky.

In that place there was no land, only blue water rippling out in every direction. And floating in the midst of the water was a house of white shell and crystal, shining with all the colors of the rainbow. Talking God and Calling God were waiting for her there. They showed her all the different rooms of her house—the rooms of dawn and the rooms of twilight, the rooms of sea and sky, the rooms of summer and autumn. Everything was perfect in the house of Changing Woman, and she ran from room to room laughing and singing. Then Talking God and Calling God said good-bye, but they instructed the twelve gods and goddesses to stay with Changing Woman for a little while longer.

For four days and four nights Changing Woman wandered through her new home without sleeping, and the twelve gods and goddesses waited to see what she would do. They knew she was thinking of something wonderful, and they stayed very quiet so as not to disturb her.

After the fourth night had passed, Changing Woman set a white shell basket on the floor and clapped her hands. "My children, some people will be made!" she cried. Then she rubbed some skin from her chest, rolled it into a small ball, and placed it in the basket. She rubbed a ball of skin from her right arm and placed it in the basket, too. Then she did the same with her left arm, and her right hand and her left hand, and her right shoulder and left shoulder. Then she covered the basket with a cloth and stepped over it four times. When she uncovered the basket, eight people stepped out, four men and four women.

She told the people to sit down, and they sat down. Then she rubbed them and brushed them until they were perfect. She gave them beautiful clothes to wear and decorated them with jewels. "Now, my children, you will be humans," she told them. She blew on them and gave them the power of speech.

"Now you can tell one another stories," she told them.

All that day Changing Woman spoke to the new people she had created. She told them about the place she had prepared for them, which is this good earth. She instructed them in how to find food and shelter, how to pray, and how to live together peacefully.

That is how Changing Woman created the first human people, the mothers and fathers of the first four clans. When morning came, she sent them forth into the new country that was prepared for them, and they traveled joyfully through the mountains and valleys of this beautiful world.

MACHA,
GODDESS OF HORSES
A CELTIC GODDESS

Macha, with her sisters Morrigan and Badb, was revered by the Celtic people of ancient Ireland. Because the Celts did not practice the art of writing, what we know of their religion and mythology must be pieced together from archaeological evidence and the fragments of their myths that were preserved as folktales by early Christian monks.

Archaeologists have found many statues of a horse goddess throughout Celtic Europe. The horse was an important symbol of fertility to the Celts. Some statues show a goddess standing beside a foal, a horn of plenty in her hand. This tale about Macha is preserved in an epic story from ancient Ireland called "The Ulster Cycle," and it shows her connection to horses. The story is set in Ulster, a county in Northern Ireland.

In ancient times in Ireland, there lived a good cattle farmer whose name was Crundchu Mac Agnoman. His wife died, leaving him four sons to raise on his own. He worked hard and did the best he could, struggling day and night to care for his children, tend his cows, and keep bread on his table. He was not an old man, but Crundchu Mac Agnoman grew haggard and careworn under the weight of his responsibilities. He smiled seldom and never laughed at all.

One cold winter evening Crundchu sat exhausted at his dinner table, rocking his

youngest baby in his arms to calm the little one's fretful tears, wondering where he would find the energy to get up and milk the cows. Suddenly the door flew open. In strode a tall and elegant lady, as lovely as a queen. Her hair was as black as a raven's feathers and hung in heavy braids down to her waist. Her eyes were the color of hyacinths, her skin as pale as the first snow of winter.

Without saying a word, she took the baby out of Crundchu's arms and settled him on her hip. Immediately the baby grew quiet and began to suck his thumb. She cleared the dishes from the table and swept the room. Laying the sleepy baby down in his cradle, she went out to the barn to milk the cows. In a short while, she was back again, a pail of steaming milk in either hand. She put the older children to bed, then built up the fire until the house was warm and cozy.

All this time Crundchu watched her openmouthed, not daring to speak. "Who are you?" he finally managed to whisper.

"My name is Macha," said the woman with a smile so brilliant the room itself seemed to throb with light.

From that day forward, Macha stayed with him. She tended the farm and cared for the children, and with her help Crundchu's farm prospered beyond his wildest dreams. No garden in Ireland grew half so many vegetables as Crundchu Mac Agnoman's. His cows produced more milk than any in Ulster. Never had the good farmer known such happiness. With Macha by his side, he seemed to bloom like the flowers in her garden. He laughed easily now and was known throughout Ulster for his hospitality and pleasant company.

Now, it was Macha's habit to leave the farm for a few hours in the afternoon, and where she went no one knew. She would finish her work and disappear into the thick wood beyond the pasture.

At first Crundchu never thought much about this, but as time passed, he began to wonder more and more about where she might be going each afternoon.

After several years of peaceful life together, Crundchu noticed that Macha would soon be having a baby. Glad as he was, he began to wonder more urgently than ever where his wife went each day with never a word about where she might be going or why. So one afternoon the farmer followed his wife as she crossed the pastures and headed for the thick wood. Although big with the child growing inside of her, she moved so swiftly that he was hardly able to keep her in view. Soon he lost sight of her altogether, but he followed the trail she'd been following herself. It wound up a steep hillside.

Huffing and puffing with the effort of the climb, he came at last to the top of the hill. The trees grew more sparsely there, and at last he broke out of the wood and looked down on a broad plain where a herd of wild horses was grazing.

Something startled the horses—perhaps they caught the scent of the man watching them—and they began to gallop across the plain. Crundchu Mac Agnoman gasped with wonder to see Macha herself, his very own wife, running before the herd. More swiftly than the wild stallion she ran, until the wild herd was no more than a blur of color in the distance.

The bewildered farmer headed home again, shaking his head and wondering to himself. Now he knew for certain his wife was no ordinary woman. But when Macha returned to the farm late in the afternoon, serene as a lake on a still summer day, he said nothing of what he had seen.

As the time for Macha to give birth drew near, an important gathering was called in Ulster. As many as could go would be there, both men and women. "I will go, too," said Crundchu to his wife.

"Don't go," she urged him. "My time is very near, and it's better if you are here when the baby is born."

But Crundchu insisted he must go with the others to Ulster.

"Very well," said Macha. "If you must go, you must. But, my husband, I beg you, say nothing of me while you are at the gathering. Our marriage cannot continue if you do."

"I will not say a word," the farmer swore.

The following week the men and women of Ulster all came to the gathering. Crundchu was there along with all the rest. It was a marvelous festival, with processions and music, and games and tournaments as well.

At the ninth hour the royal chariot was brought out onto the fairground, and the king's horses won all the races that day. The bards sang praises to the king and queen, the poets and the Druids, the king's household, his people, and the whole assembly. "Never before have we seen such horses as those that pull the king's chariot. In all Ireland there is not a swifter pair!" cried the people.

"My wife runs more swiftly than those two," said Crundchu without thinking, and everyone heard him.

The king, who was sitting nearby, heard him as well. "Seize that man!" he cried. "Hold him until his wife can be brought to the contest."

The king's guards tied up Crundchu, and a messenger was sent to bring Macha to the gathering. When the messenger arrived at the farm, he found Macha ready to give birth that very day. She was doubled over with the pangs of labor. Nonetheless, the messenger insisted she come to the gathering. If she refused, her husband would be put to death for his boasting.

Macha accompanied the messenger to the gathering and went before the king.

"What do you want of me?" she asked him.

"Your husband claims that you can run faster than my two horses. If you wish to prove him right, run in contest with them now. Otherwise I shall have him put to death," answered the king.

"Not now!" cried Macha as another labor pain seized her.

"Take out your swords and hack that man to death," the king commanded his guards.

Macha regarded the bystanders. "Help me," she pleaded. "Do not make me do this thing. Or at least let me wait a little until my baby is born."

But the crowd stood silent. Not one person spoke in her defense.

"Then shame on you who have shown so little respect for me," she cried, and her voice rang out across the assembly ground like a clap of thunder. "Because you have shown no pity for me, I will have no pity on you. Do you not know me? I am Macha, daughter of the ocean's son. Bring the horses beside me."

The horses were brought to her, and the race began. Macha ran before them as swiftly as the wind, easily outdistancing them. When she had crossed the finish line, with the king's horses far behind her, she gave birth then and there to twins, a boy and a girl. Then she rose and faced the crowd, towering above them in all her power.

"From this day forward, the shame you have forced on me will be a shame on your heads. When a time of oppression falls on you, every man born in this province will become as weak as a woman who is ready to give birth, powerless to act against the forces ranged against him. For nine times nine generations it will be so."

Taking her babies, one under each arm, she gave a wild cry of sorrow. Every man who heard her cry was struck by a strange weakness, so that he had no more strength in his limbs than a woman in childbirth. Then Macha and her twins disappeared, and never again were they seen in Ireland.

SEDNA, WOMAN OF THE SEA

SUPREME DEITY OF THE INUIT PEOPLE

Sedna, Woman of the Sea, is the supreme deity of the traditional Inuit people. According to the old stories, she lives in the depths of the ocean, the mistress of all sea creatures. When she wishes, she sends her animals swimming up to the ocean's surface, where they can be hunted for food. But if Sedna grows angry, she keeps her animals inside her house. Then there is nothing to hunt, and the people go hungry. When this happens, the *angaguk*—the Eskimo shaman—must journey in a trance to Sedna's home beneath the waves and comb her hair for her. Only then will she release some of her animals so that people have food once more.

Long ago, at the beginning of all things, there lived a young woman more beautiful than any other, before or since. Not only was she beautiful, she was also very proud. Her name was Sedna, and she lived alone with her father, for her mother had died giving birth to her. She had thick black hair that fell to her waist, and nothing pleased her more than to spend endless hours staring out to sea as she combed her long hair.

Every young man in Sedna's village was madly in love with her, for she was so beautiful. One by one they came to her and begged her to marry, but she refused

them all. Some of the men were handsome, others were skilled hunters, while others were kind and gentle and knew how to care for a woman. But none of these men seemed right for her. She wanted something different, though she didn't know what. So Sedna stayed by herself, waiting for whatever wonderful thing might come her way someday.

In early spring a stranger came to the village. He was handsome as handsome can be, with skin like bronze and hair as thick and shiny as Sedna's own. He walked so lightly that it seemed his feet barely touched the ground, and he wore dark glasses made of walrus tusks so that none could see his eyes. He walked straight up to Sedna and smiled at her. "You will be my wife," he said.

Sedna tossed her hair and turned away. "I don't think so," she answered him. But her heart beat quickly, and she longed to look into the eyes of the mysterious stranger.

The next day, he came to her as she sat alone on a high cliff staring out to sea.

"Come with me, Sedna," the stranger urged in a voice as sweet as honey. "Come with me across the sea. I have a beautiful home there, more beautiful than any in this village. You shall sleep on soft bearskins and wear clothes of white feathers. How beautiful you are, my dear one. Far too beautiful for this small place. Come away with me and be my wife."

Sedna smiled at the stranger and tossed her hair. She didn't say yes, but she didn't say no.

On the following day the stranger approached her once more.

"Oh, Sedna," he said with a sigh, "if only you would marry me and come to my home across the sea. My people would honor you as if you were a queen. You would have reindeer meat to eat every day of the year. How happy we would be, my dearest one. Tomorrow I must leave your village and journey back to my homeland. Say you will come with me."

Sedna looked down at her hands, then out to the sea. Her fingers itched to tear off the man's dark glasses and look into his eyes. She didn't say yes, but she didn't say no.

The next day was set for the stranger's departure. Early in the morning Sedna climbed up to her spot on the cliff and waited for him to find her. Soon he came and sat down beside her. He began to sing to her in a language she didn't understand. The strange, sweet music made her feel sad and hollow inside. She longed to gaze into the stranger's eyes and see herself reflected there.

"Do you know what I was singing, my darling?" the stranger murmured when his song was finished.

Sedna shook her head mutely.

"I was singing of how much I love you, and how lonely I will be on my long journey back to my homeland. I will think of you day and night, my Sedna, my darling. You have stolen my heart, and I fear I shall never get it back again. Ah, my sweet, if only you would come with me. How happy you could make me."

The stranger stood and turned to leave her, but Sedna put out her hand and stopped him. The desire to see into his eyes overwhelmed her—she could not possibly let him leave without her.

"I will come," she whispered.

The stranger insisted that they must be married at once and leave that very day. The journey to his homeland was a long and dangerous one, and they couldn't risk the bad weather setting in before they had reached their destination.

Sedna hurried to tell her father the news. Her father was not happy to hear of her decision. He begged her not to go so far away with this strange man, about whom they knew nothing. But Sedna was determined, and since she had already refused to marry every young man in the area, he realized this was his last chance to see his daughter wed.

"Go safely, my daughter," Sedna's father said at last. "When the spring comes once more, I myself will travel across the sea to visit you. Until then, good-bye."

So Sedna set out to sea in her new husband's kayak. The journey was long and difficult, but after many weeks they sighted a small island whose rocky shores were stained white with the droppings of fulmars, the noisy seabirds that wheeled in circles over their heads. Sedna's husband shouted with joy.

"At last, my dear! We are home!"

Sedna looked at her husband in disbelief. "This is your home?" she cried. "This is the place you spoke so highly of? Why, there's nothing on this island but a flock of noisy fulmars."

Her husband threw back his head and began laughing like a madman. He laughed so hard that his walrus-tusk glasses slipped from his face, and Sedna saw that his eyes were beady red circles. Slowly his laugh changed from the laugh of a man to the harsh cry of a fulmar; his arms became wings; his lovely bronze skin sprouted white feathers. Sedna realized with horror that the handsome man she'd married so hastily was, in fact, a fulmar, which had tricked her into marriage by disguising himself as a man.

From that day on, Sedna lived a miserable existence. The fulmars kept her in a smelly tent made of fish skins and gave her nothing but fish bones to eat. They laughed at her because she could not fly, and pecked at her whenever she complained. Her husband's red eyes filled her with revulsion, so that she could not bear to look at him. The only thing that kept Sedna from utter despair was the thought that when the winter was over, her father would come, as he had promised, and rescue her from her hideous new family.

At last the harsh arctic winter gave way to spring. The ice that bound up the sea began to melt, and the waves broke once more on the shores of the fulmars' island. Sedna knew that soon her father would arrive. Every day she scanned the horizon anxiously, hoping for the first glimpse of his kayak.

Just when she had begun to fear that her father had forgotten his promise to visit her, she saw his boat appear from behind an iceberg. It was afternoon, and the fulmars were all out fishing over the open sea. Sedna waved her arms wildly to attract his attention, and soon her father was paddling toward her with a worried frown upon his face.

As soon as his kayak drew close to the shore, Sedna waded into the icy water and climbed inside. She told her father what had happened, and she begged him to take her away.

Her father had been anticipating a warm welcome from his son-in-law, with a good meal of reindeer meat after his long journey. Now he shook his head in disgust.

"You foolish girl!" he shouted angrily. "I warned you not to marry a stranger. You could have had any man you wanted, but you had to choose a fulmar for a husband!"

"Father, I'm sorry!" Sedna cried in desperation. "But please take me away from this horrible place before the fulmars come back and try to stop me from leaving!"

Reluctantly her father turned the boat around and began to paddle back in the direction from which he'd come. The sea was calm, and soon they were a good distance from the fulmars' island.

In the meantime, the fulmar returned home from fishing and found his beautiful wife was gone. At once he suspected that her father had come for her, and the bird flew out over the ocean to try to catch her. After many hours of searching, he spied at last the little kayak bobbing on the sea below him. Swooping down, he called to Sedna's father to return his wife to him.

Sedna's father pretended not to hear and kept on paddling as fast as he could.

"Give her back, give her back," croaked the bird. But Sedna's father paid no notice, and Sedna herself huddled in the boat and covered her face with her shiny black hair.

Now the fulmar grew angry. He beat his enormous wings in the air, and a cold wind began to blow from the north. A dark cloud covered the pale midnight sun. Rain and hail began to fall. Waves as high as mountains rose up, threatening to capsize the fragile kayak.

"Give me back my wife! Give me back my wife!" screeched the bird. The waves rose higher and higher.

In mortal terror, certain that both he and his daughter would soon be thrown into a watery grave, Sedna's father seized her by the hair and flung her overboard.

"She's yours," he shouted up to the fulmar. "Let me live!"

But Sedna refused to surrender herself and clung with all her strength to the edge of her father's boat. Another vast wave lifted them high into the air, tossing the tiny kayak this way and that. Still Sedna clung fast to the boat. Her father took out his knife and cut off some of her fingers, yet Sedna still managed to cling on. He cut off the rest of her fingers, and still she clung on. Finally he cut off her hands, and with nothing to grip with, the beautiful young woman sank beneath the waves. Immediately the sea grew calm, and Sedna's father paddled out of sight.

Down, down, down sank Sedna, down to the bottom of the sea. But she did not die. As she sank, her shiny black hair grew even longer, drifting out across all the oceans of the world to become seaweed. Her severed fingers were transformed into seals and walruses and salmon. Her severed hands became whales. These animals of the sea circled lovingly about her, accompanying her down to the ocean's floor.

There, in the deepest depths of the ocean, Sedna found a house waiting for her. A bridge as narrow as a knife's edge led up to it, and a wheel of fire spun before it. The house was as clear and shining as crystal, a house of many rooms, shimmering with all the colors of the rainbow. Outside the house burned a lamp whose well of oil is never empty.

In this house of splendor lives Sedna, the goddess of the sea. She has everything her heart desires, and her animals are always with her. Only one thing troubles her: Because she has no hands, she cannot comb her wonderful long hair, and sometimes it becomes unbearably tangled. But if any Inuit is brave enough to journey down to her palace and comb out her hair, she rewards all human beings by sending the sea creatures up to the surface of the water, where they can be hunted for food.

KUAN YIN, THE COMPASSIONATE
A BUDDHIST GODDESS

Kuan Yin, a Buddhist goddess, is especially revered in China, even to this day. Her name is translated as "She Who Listens to the World's Sounds." This is because of her great compassion for the suffering of all humankind. One of the legends of Kuan Yin tells that the day on which she was scheduled to enter heaven, she turned away from the gates of paradise because she heard the cries of human misery below. She refuses to enter heaven until all suffering has ended in the world. Kuan Yin's name is evoked in times of need, for she is known to rescue those who are in danger or are very ill. She also gives comfort to the dying and brings children to women who desire to have babies. The following myth tells the story of how the girl Miao Shan became the goddess Kuan Yin.

Long ago in China there lived an ambitious ruler named Miao Chuang. He waged war with all his neighbors and defeated them, until he ruled over a vast empire. But during all the years of war his people suffered greatly and many lives were lost.

Miao Chuang had three daughters, but no sons. He feared he would die and the kingdom for which he had fought so bitterly would be lost without a son to carry on his name. So he decided to marry his daughters to worthy men and then choose from among them a successor to the throne.

The three princesses grew like flowers in their father's palace. The two older sisters, Miao Ch'ing and Miao Yin, delighted in palace life and spent their days planning new festivities and ways to amuse themselves. But the youngest daughter, Miao Shan, was different from her sisters. She was quiet and serious and enjoyed spending time alone in the palace gardens much more than gossiping with the courtiers or trying on new clothes.

It came time for the three girls to be married. The older sisters were happy when their father found rich and powerful husbands for them. But Miao Shan surprised everyone by declaring she had no wish to marry at all. Instead, she longed to become a Buddhist nun.

Her father was shocked and angry. "Whoever heard of a king's daughter becoming a nun? The idea is absurd! I will find a great scholar for you to marry, someone to rule in my place once I am gone. Don't talk to me about a religious life. Are you forgetting that you're a princess?"

Miao Shan remained unmoved by her father's fury. "My only desire in this life is to heal humanity of its ills, of war and poverty, sickness and hunger," she told him.

"You are mad!" shouted the emperor. "Go to your chambers and stay there until you've recovered your senses."

So Miao Shan stayed shut in her rooms, fasting and praying. Being shut away from palace life didn't bother her at all. In fact, she was glad to have this time for quiet meditation. Every day her mother, the queen, came to her and begged her to change her mind. But the weeks passed and Miao Shan listened only to her heart.

At last she said to her mother, "Please try to understand this. My greatest wish is to join the nuns in the Temple of the White Bird and study Buddhism. Try to persuade my father that this is the best way."

Convinced that Miao Shan would never willingly consent to marriage, the queen pleaded with Miao Chuang to allow their daughter to become a nun. At last he consented. But he sent word to the nuns that they must do everything in their power to dissuade Miao Shan from her intention to remain with them. If Miao Shan insisted on joining the religious order, the emperor warned, he would have the temple burned to the ground.

When Miao Shan arrived at the Temple of the White Bird, she was put to work in the kitchen and ordered to prepare food for the entire community. Although she was a princess and had never had to work before, she took on the task with a good heart. The nuns kept her busy from morning until late at night, cooking, cleaning, chopping wood, and fetching water. And Miao Shan was content to be of service and devote herself to the Buddha.

One day a wild tiger wandered out of the forest and came to the kitchen door. On his back was a load of wood. He knelt down beside Miao Shan and allowed her to take the wood from his back. Then he disappeared, but each day after that he returned carrying a load of wood for the gentle princess so that she wouldn't have to carry it herself. Another day a heavenly dragon flew down from the sky and dug a well beside the kitchen door so that Miao Shan would not have to walk to the spring to fetch water. And the birds of the forest began to collect vegetables for Miao Shan so that she would not have to run to the garden and collect them. In this way she easily completed all the tasks the nuns set for her and still had time to study and pray.

Word of these miracles reached the court of Miao Chuang, and he was outraged. He sent his soldiers to burn down the nunnery and force his daughter to return to the palace. When the soldiers arrived at the Temple of the White Bird, they surrounded it and started a blazing fire. The terrified nuns huddled together inside the temple, awaiting death.

"This is all your fault," one of the nuns accused Miao Shan. "You have brought destruction on us all."

"It's true," said Miao Shan. "I alone am responsible for this calamity."

Then she knelt down and prayed to heaven to protect the innocent nuns from the fire. At the end of her prayers, she took a bamboo hairpin from her hair and punctured the roof of her mouth with it. Then she spat the flowing blood toward the sky. Immediately, great storm clouds gathered over the nunnery and soaked it with rain, extinguishing the fire.

The princess left the temple and surrendered herself to the soldiers. Frightened by the strange events they had just witnessed, the soldiers wrapped her in chains and carried her back to the court.

Miao Shan was brought before the emperor in disgrace. Her father regarded her coldly. He could not believe that his own daughter would dare to disobey him.

"Do you still refuse to marry?" he demanded.

Miao Shan looked down at her feet. "Forgive me, Father," she said. "I wish I could obey you, but it is impossible. I cannot return to the life of the palace."

"Then you will die for your disobedience," decreed Miao Chuang, and he turned away from his daughter and refused to look at her again.

On the following day Miao Shan was led to the place of execution. The princess walked with her head held high, her face radiant with joy. At the palace gates she saw her mother and her two older sisters weeping pitifully. "Dear sisters, dear mother, don't weep for me," she called to them. "Today I leave this world for a better one. It is the happiest day of my life."

As Miao Shan neared the place of execution the sky grew overcast and dark, but all who looked on Miao Shan saw that she was surrounded by a brilliant white light. When the sword of the executioner fell on her neck, the weapon shattered into a thousand pieces, and Miao Shan remained unharmed. Then, the executioner thrust at her with a spear, but the spear broke into shards. Finally, he was forced to strangle her with a silken cord. As Miao Shan fell lifeless to the ground a huge tiger leaped onto the execution ground and dragged her body into the forest.

Meanwhile, Miao Shan's soul was carried away on a cloud and taken to a place without mountains or trees, sun or moon or stars, a place without people or animals or anything living, a place with neither sound nor color.

"What is this terrible place?" Miao Shan cried.

Immediately a strange man appeared before her. "Welcome, Miao Shan, to the land of the dead," he said. "Since you were a disobedient daughter, I will now lead you to the king of all the hells."

As Miao Shan followed the guide down a bleak road she gradually became aware of heartbreaking moans and cries coming from either side of her. Through the swirls of evil-smelling fog, she began to distinguish faces contorted by pain and grief.

"Who are these people, and why are they crying?" she demanded of her guide.

"These are the souls of the condemned," he told her.

"Then I must pray for them," she exclaimed, and knelt in the road and began to pray with all her heart. As she prayed, the foul mists of hell dispersed and lotus flowers sprang up all around her.

The king of hells was dismayed to see his domain transformed into a paradise of peace and joy. For the sake of justice, there must be a hell as well as a heaven. If Miao Shan remained, there would no longer be a hell. So he sent a message to the guide directing him to escort Miao Shan back to the land of the living.

Miao Shan was led across the river that separates the land of the living from the underworld, and reentered her body. She woke to find herself lying under a pine tree in the middle of the forest. She looked up and saw the tiger, still standing beside her body.

When the tiger saw that Miao Shan lived once more, he instructed her to climb onto his back. Swift and silent, he carried the gentle princess across China to the far island of P'u T'o. There, Miao Shan devoted herself to prayer and meditation. During this time she worked many miracles. When a sick man came to see her, he would soon find himself healed. If a woman wished to have a child but was unable to conceive, a visit to Miao Shan cured her barrenness. People who suffered from grief or feelings of remorse for a past ill deed needed only to speak of their troubles to Miao Shan to feel at peace. And when she stood on the rocky shores of P'u T'o, even the most violent storm could not rock the boats of islanders, so that she was especially loved by sailors and fishermen.

After nine years on P'u T'o, Miao Shan had reached the height of perfection. All the gods and goddesses of heaven recognized her as a divine being, a Buddha. She was given the name Kuan Yin.

Meanwhile, ever since ordering his daughter's execution the emperor Miao Chuang had been afflicted with a terrible illness. His entire body was covered with sores. Miao Chuang consulted every healer he could find, but no one was able to cure him of the agonizing disease. Finally a Buddhist priest told him that he could only be healed by medicine made from the arms and eyes of a living person who was completely free from anger. When Miao Chuang heard this, he despaired of ever finding a cure, for surely no such person existed in the world. But the priest assured the king that such a person did indeed exist and would willingly sacrifice her arms and eyes in order to save him.

Then the priest sent word to Kuan Yin that her father had need of her, and the princess immediately returned to Miao Chuang's palace. When she heard what was required, she showed no hesitation but seized a knife and cut off her arms and gouged out her eyes to give to her father. Then the flesh of the goddess was ground into an ointment that cured the king of his painful sores.

When Miao Chuang had recovered, he begged to be shown the selfless person willing to sacrifice arms and eyes on his behalf. When he found that it was his own daughter whom he had treated so heartlessly, he fell on his knees and begged her forgiveness.

Kuan Yin laughed merrily, and as she laughed, a thousand arms grew from the place where she had cut off her arms. And where she had gouged out her eyes, she now had a thousand eyes.

"Do not ask my forgiveness, dear father," she said gently. "What's done is done. Through helping you I have become everything I yearned to be."

Then a dazzling light surrounded the goddess, so bright that the king was forced to look away. When he raised his eyes to look at her once more, she had disappeared. But she has never left this world, and if anyone is in great need and calls for Kuan Yin, she will return.

ISIS, MISTRESS OF LIFE AND DEATH
AN ANCIENT EGYPTIAN GODDESS

Isis was the most powerful and the most widely known goddess of the ancient Egyptians. She was worshiped for more than three thousand years. Temples were built in her honor, not only in Egypt, but also throughout the Mediterranean, in Rome and Greece, and as far east as India. For the ancient Egyptians the myth of Isis and Osiris was associated with the annual flooding of the Nile River. Here, Isis is seen as a fertility goddess, representing the fertile earth. It is through her union with Osiris, who represents the Nile River, that all life is made possible.

Long ago, at the beginning of the world, Nut, the sky goddess, and Geb, the god of the earth, gave birth to four children: Osiris, Isis, Seth, and Nepthys. Following the ways of the gods, the four children married one another. Isis and Osiris, who had loved each other even in their mother's womb, were married to each other, and Seth married his sister Nepthys.

Osiris loved humankind, and he became the first king of Egypt, with Isis ruling as his queen. He taught his people to plant grain and cultivate it, so that hunger disappeared

from the land. He taught them to honor the gods and gave them laws to govern with justice. Then leaving Isis to rule Egypt in his place, he wandered throughout the world, sharing his skills and teaching his wisdom to all humanity.

But Isis missed her husband day and night. At last she sent him a message, reminding him of her love and begging him to come back to her. When Osiris received the message, he was filled with longing for his queen and quickly returned to Egypt. The people were overjoyed and welcomed their king with delight.

Seth saw how the people of Egypt revered his brother, Osiris. He saw that they sang his praises and paid homage to him, not simply because he was a god, but also because they loved him. He became tortured with jealousy. Seth wanted to rule as king in his brother's place, but he kept his desire hidden from Isis and Osiris.

Quietly Seth gathered together men who were greedy for power and felt no loyalty toward Osiris. With seventy-two conspirators Seth plotted to kill the king of Egypt and seize the throne for himself. He secretly ordered that a coffin be built that fitted his brother's measurements exactly. The coffin was fashioned from gold and encrusted with jewels, a thing of great beauty. Then he prepared a magnificent banquet and invited his brother to attend.

Suspecting nothing, Osiris came to Seth's banquet. He ate the fine food his brother's household had prepared and spent many hours playing music, singing, and dancing. In the midst of the festivities, Seth presented the beautiful coffin to all of his guests. He declared that anyone who could fit perfectly inside the coffin should have it as a gift. Everyone admired the beautiful coffin, and one guest after another tried to fit himself inside the narrow chest without success. Finally Osiris himself lay down inside the coffin. At this instant the seventy-two conspirators rushed forward and slammed the lid of the coffin down on Osiris' face. Ignoring his cries, they sealed it shut and poured molten lead over it. Then they carried the coffin to the river and allowed it to float away to the sea.

Soon Isis heard the news that Osiris was dead. She wept so hard that her tears flooded the Nile. She cut off her hair and covered her head with ashes. Then she set out to find the body of her husband.

For many months Isis wandered along the banks of the Nile, and everywhere she went, she asked if anyone had found her husband's body. At last some children told her that one morning they had seen a group of men carry a shining box to the river's edge. They had watched as the golden chest floated away toward the sea.

Isis continued her search, asking everyone she met if they had seen or heard of the golden chest. In this way she learned that a golden coffin had washed ashore at Byblos and embedded itself in the trunk of an erica tree. The tree continued to grow, enfolding the coffin in its bark, and when the king of Byblos heard of this marvel, he ordered that the tree be cut down and made into a pillar to hold up the roof of his palace.

Isis knew at once that this must be the coffin that contained Osiris' body. She disguised herself as a poor old woman dressed in rags and journeyed to Byblos. There she met some of the queen's attendants, who were swimming in the sea. She offered to braid their hair, and when she touched them, she gave off such a wonderful scent that the girls were spellbound. The fragrance of Isis clung to their hair and clothes, and when the queen of Byblos smelled this perfume, she demanded to meet the woman who had braided her servants' hair. The girls ran back to the beach to fetch Isis, and brought her to their mistress. The queen was delighted by the woman's heavenly smell, her beauty, and her gentleness. She made Isis nursemaid to her infant son.

Isis cared for the little boy and soon grew to love him. She decided to make him immortal. Whenever he was hungry, she gave him her fingertip to suck on. And at night when everyone in the palace was sleeping, she built a fire and passed the baby through the flames to burn away his mortality. Then she turned herself into a swallow and flew around the pillar that contained Osiris' casket, crying for her lost love.

One night the queen of Byblos happened to wake in the middle of the night. Disturbed by strange dreams, she wandered into the palace hall and saw Isis holding her baby boy in the fire. The queen began to scream in horror. Certain he would burn to death, she grabbed the little boy out of Isis' arms. Then she saw that her child was unharmed.

The queen stared at the old woman she'd taken to be a nursemaid with fear and wonder. "Who are you?" she whispered.

Isis shook off her ragged disguise, revealing herself as a goddess. "I am Isis, foolish woman," she said. "I had intended to make your child immortal and a god. Because of your fear, he will remain mortal and die as all men must. Now I, too, must go. I have come seeking the body of my husband, Osiris, who is buried in the casket of this pillar."

With the king's permission Isis removed the coffin from the erica tree. Clasping it in her arms, she wailed so loudly that one of the king's sons heard her and died of fright. She put the coffin on board a ship and sailed home to Egypt.

Once in Egypt, Isis took the coffin deep into the swamps of the delta, where no one could find it. She lifted the lid and looked at her husband's corpse. Grief shook her like a great storm raging inside her. She fell on the body of Osiris and kissed him. As her tears washed over his body a miracle occurred. Osiris was dead, but Isis conceived his son. In secret she gave birth to a baby boy and named him Horus.

Now, Seth believed that the body of Osiris was gone from the land of Egypt and no one could challenge his right to the throne. But one day he was out hunting wild boar, and he chased the boar into the swampy delta of the Nile. By chance he discovered the body of Osiris, lying in its golden coffin. Furious, he tore the corpse into fourteen pieces and scattered them up and down the length of the country.

When Isis heard what he had done, she went once more in search of her husband's body. Together with her sister, Nepthys, and the god Anubis, who guards the bridge between the land of the living and the land of the dead, she built a boat of papyrus and sailed down the Nile. When she had found all the parts of her husband's body, she embalmed him and performed magic rites over him. Through the power of Isis' magic and the strength of her faithfulness, Osiris was revived from the dead.

But he did not stay on earth. He went to rule as lord of the dead, and there he remains to this day and forevermore. When the dead leave this world, they join Osiris in his glorious kingdom of eternity, a land with neither hunger nor war, where all live in peace and joy under his benevolent reign.

Yet the spirit of Osiris lived on earth through his son, Horus. While Horus was still young and weak, Isis hid him far from the jealous reach of her wicked brother Seth. She guarded him as fiercely as a mother hawk. Day and night she cared for him, until at last he had grown to his full strength. Then she brought him to the court of the gods.

Isis knelt before the mighty sun god, Re, dispenser of justice and ruler of all the gods, and begged him to accept Horus as the rightful king of Egypt. But Seth challenged Horus' claim to the throne, declaring that he was not strong enough to be king. Horus and Seth fought many terrible battles. Isis remained by Horus' side and used her magic and wisdom to help him in his struggle. In the end Horus was victorious. The company of the gods recognized him as king, and Seth was vanquished.

For thousands of years, Isis remained on earth, guarding over Horus and his descendants, the pharaohs of ancient Egypt. Yet she also ruled at Osiris' side in the afterlife, as queen of heaven. She knew the secret of both death and life, and brought comfort and assistance to those who called her name in times of need.

IX CHEL, THE MOON GODDESS
AN ANCIENT MAYAN GODDESS

The ancient Mayans revered the moon goddess, who has many names but is often called Ix Chel, which means "Lady Rainbow." She is also the goddess of water and of weaving, one of the most important activities of ancient Mayan women. As she weaves her cosmic tapestry, Ix Chel creates order in the universe. As moon goddess, she regulates women's fertility and gives strength to women in childbirth. In Mayan hieroglyphic texts she is pictured wearing a serpent headdress. The story of the moon goddess's marriage to the sun god is preserved in Mayan folklore.

There was a girl, and she was a skilled weaver, as fine a weaver as ever there was. She lived with her grandfather, and every day she took her loom out onto the patio to do her weaving. Sun saw her sitting there. She was very beautiful, and the cloth she wove was the finest cloth he'd ever seen. He decided to court this lovely young woman. To impress her, he went hunting and caught a deer, then walked by her house carrying the deer on his shoulders. The girl saw him walk by and admired the large deer he was carrying.

The next day Sun wanted to see the girl again. But deer were scarce and he couldn't find another one, so he stuffed the same deer's body with ashes and carried it by the girl's house again. Every day he did this. The girl was very impressed by what a skilled hunter he was. But her grandfather was suspicious and told her to throw water on the path be-

fore their house. The next day when Sun came walking by with his deer full of ashes, he slipped on the muddy path and fell. The deerskin burst and covered Sun with ashes, and the girl started laughing at him. Embarrassed, Sun turned himself into a hummingbird and tried to fly away, but the girl told her grandfather to shoot the hummingbird with his blowgun. The old man shot the bird and stunned it. Then the girl took the bird into her room. All day long she stroked the little bird, admiring its colorful feathers.

At night the hummingbird revived, and Sun resumed his human shape. He talked to the girl and persuaded her to run away with him. But she knew her grandfather would be angry and come after her if she tried to run away. Her grandfather had a magic crystal ball in which he could see everything, and he would look in the crystal and know where to find them. Then he would kill them with his blowgun. So Sun put ashes in her grandfather's crystal ball, to cloud it. He put chili pepper in her grandfather's blowgun. At last the girl felt safe, and she agreed to leave with her lover.

Soon after they'd left the house, the grandfather woke from strange dreams. He felt that something was wrong. He went into the girl's room and found her gone. When he looked in his crystal ball, he saw nothing but misty swirls. Then the grandfather called his friend Chac, the volcano god, and asked him to find the young couple and slay them. Chac found the young couple paddling down the river in a canoe. He sent a lightning bolt to kill them. Sun saw the lightning bolt coming and quickly turned himself into a turtle to escape the blow. He turned the girl into a crab. The lightning bolt missed the turtle, but it struck the crab. The girl's body exploded, and all her blood flowed from her.

Sun saw the girl's blood spilled on the water. He called to the dragonflies and begged them to help. The dragonflies collected every drop of the girl's blood. They stored her blood in thirteen hollow logs. Now Sun waited. He waited thirteen days. On the thirteenth day he opened up the logs. Out of the first twelve logs came snakes. They slithered away in every direction, and to this day they are everywhere on earth. Out of the thirteenth log emerged the girl. At first she was very small. But a magic deer came and leaped over her four times. She grew big and bright. She was Ix Chel, the moon. Sun asked her to marry him, and she consented. Together they rose to the sky, shining gloriously.

Sun built a house in the sky world for his new wife. Sun's brother Xulab, the morning star, came to live with them. Ix Chel loved the fiery sun, but she soon came to love his slender brother as well. Sun grew jealous of Xulab and Ix Chel. It seemed that every time he turned his back, they were together. He began to rage at her constantly. They were always fighting and never slept. The world was too bright. Finally Ix Chel grew tired from all the fighting. She left the sky and went to live with the king of the vultures.

Sun could not bear to live without his Ix Chel, and he was determined to get her back again. Once again he took his deerskin, and this time he climbed inside it. Then he lay on the desert floor pretending to be a dead deer. Some vultures came and carried the deer carcass back to their king. When Sun arrived at the vulture king's palace, he slipped from the deerskin and went in search of Ix Chel. He found her at her weaving, and begged and pleaded with her to come back to the sky with him.

Ix Chel relented and returned to Sun's home. For a time all went well, but then Sun became jealous again. He thought his brother Chocl, the cloud god, must be in love with Ix Chel. When Sun went looking for Ix Chel, Chocl was always standing in front of her, covering her beautiful light. Sun began to beat Ix Chel, hoping to mark her so that she wouldn't be so beautiful and attract the other gods. His beatings scarred her perfect body. Ix Chel knew she had to leave the house of Sun. He was still her husband, but they couldn't live together. This time she knew she would never come back again.

Every day Sun still roams the sky looking for Ix Chel, but he can never find her. She only comes out when he is sleeping. As soon as she spies her jealous husband, she slips away again. Sometimes she disappears for days on end, and the night is dark. But Ix Chel cannot help herself—she is too beautiful to hide away forever. She always returns to shine for us in all her glory.

AMATERASU, THE SUN GODDESS
SUPREME SHINTO DEITY

Amaterasu is the supreme deity of the Japanese Shinto religion. Her name means "Great Shining Heavenly Brightness." Through her actions the universe is granted order and fertility. She is also revered as the ancestor of the Japanese emperor. The myth of Amaterasu's encounter with her brother, Susanowo, describes the beginning of the emperor's ancestral heritage. Traditionally, the emperor was believed to be the direct descendant of the gods and goddesses who were born when Susanowo and Amaterasu fought.

In the beginning there was nothing: no land, no sea, no sky. Then the earth and sky began to separate, and the gods were born in heaven. Izanagi and Izanami, the first mother and father, were sent down from heaven to prepare the earth for humans to live there. Together they made the land and the sea, the islands and mountains and rivers and trees.

Izanagi and Izanami regarded the beautiful world they had created. Then they decided to make something wonderful, a marvelous being who would rule the universe. That is how they gave birth to Amaterasu, goddess of the sun. From the moment she was born, she shone so brightly that all the world was illuminated. Izanagi and Izanami were filled with joy.

"We have had many children together," said Izanami, "but none of them are equal to this beautiful baby."

"Yes," agreed Izanagi, "this baby is by far the best of all that we have created. We must not keep her here with us too long but send her at once up to heaven and entrust her with the affairs of heaven."

With these words Izanagi took off his necklace of jewels and hung it around Amaterasu's neck. Then he sent her up to the sky. At that time heaven and earth were not very far apart, and it was easy for Amaterasu to climb up the sky pillar into heaven. Once there, she shone more brightly than ever, and all the heavenly gods were full of rejoicing to have her with them.

Amaterasu had a brother named Susanowo. From the time he was born, Susanowo was always weeping and wailing. Nothing made him happy. Izanagi told him to rule over the ocean. But Susanowo was too angry to rule properly. His tantrums made enormous tidal waves that destroyed the islands. His weeping and wailing caused typhoons and hurricanes to form. Everywhere he went, Susanowo brought destruction and turmoil with him. At last Izanagi became tired of his behavior and sent him off to the land of the dead.

"Very well," said Susanowo. "I will leave this earth and go to dwell in the land of the dead. But first give me permission to say good-bye to my sister in heaven, the shining Amaterasu."

Izanagi gave his son permission, and Susanowo began climbing the sky pillar up to heaven. When he arrived in heaven, the first thing he saw were the emerald green rice fields Amaterasu had planted, stretching across the entire plain of heaven. At the sight of his sister's fine rice fields, Susanowo was filled with jealous rage. He flooded the fields with foul waters. He filled the ditches with waste. He poisoned the soil so that nothing good could ever grow there. Not content with ruining his sister's rice fields, he went to her palace and ransacked it, spreading filth everywhere. He went to the hall where the heavenly goddesses were weaving silken clothes. Jumping onto the roof of the hall, he tore off the roof tiles and threw the rotting carcass of a dead horse down onto the goddesses weaving below, so that some of them were thrown onto their shuttles and crushed to death.

When Amaterasu first saw the havoc her brother was wreaking, she tried to make excuses for him. When he ruined her rice fields, she said that he had only been trying to help her harvest the rice and hadn't understood how much damage he was doing. When he ransacked her palace, she said that he had been drunk and unaware of the destruction. But when he caused the death of the lovely weaving goddesses, she was appalled. In grief and disgust she closed herself in a dark cave and refused to come out.

Now all the gods and goddesses were frightened and distressed, for without the sun goddess both heaven and earth were thrown into darkness. They had to do all their work by candlelight, and many tragedies occurred because no one could see properly. Finally the eight hundred gods and goddesses of heaven assembled at the mouth of the cave where Amaterasu had hidden herself. They wanted to find some way to make her come out.

After much discussion they finally conceived of a plan. First, they wove beautiful new clothes for one another and made many musical instruments and spears and swords from precious metals. The god and goddess of metalsmithing fashioned a huge mirror in the shape of the sun. They set the mirror in front of the cave. Finally, they brought all the roosters in heaven to the mouth of the cave and ordered them to crow without stopping.

Then all the gods and goddesses of heaven began to jingle their spears and swords, to sing and make music. One of the goddesses jumped up on a wooden tub and started dancing, and her dance was so funny that all the gods and goddesses started to laugh, which was a wonderful sound indeed.

When Amaterasu heard the eight hundred gods and goddesses of heaven laughing, she was astonished. She thought they should be weeping and wailing now that everything was dark. She pushed aside the rock that barred the entrance to her cave just a crack and peeked outside.

"Why are you laughing? Why are you singing and dancing?" she asked the gods and goddesses.

"Come out! Come out!" cried the eight hundred gods and goddesses.

"We are so happy, for we have found one who is even more beautiful than you," called the dancing goddess. "Come and look at her."

While she was speaking, the other gods and goddesses held the mirror before the entrance to the cave so that Amaterasu could see her own reflection. How lovely she was! Full of amazement, the sun goddess crept out of the cave so that she could gaze into the mirror.

As soon as she was all the way out, the gods and goddesses pushed back the rock and jammed it so tightly into the mouth of the cave that no one has ever been able to move it again. Then they took Amaterasu by the hand and led her to the new palace they had built for her. They gave her beautiful silken robes to wear. They showered her with jewels and flowers. They beseeched her never to shut herself away again.

When the universe felt once more the warmth of the sun and saw her dazzling light spread out across all of heaven and earth, the gods rejoiced. They saw that all was finally as it should be. Then they agreed that Susanowo must leave forever. They cut off his beard and forced him to pay a heavy fine. Then they drove him from the sky.

But Susanowo began to climb back up again. "If I must leave forever, I must see my sister again face-to-face!" he shouted. "I will never leave unless I can see her!"

The sea foamed and raged. The mountains and rivers shook. The hills groaned aloud, and every land and country quaked as Susanowo climbed the sky pillar back to heaven. From high in her heavenly palace, Amaterasu heard him coming. She tied back her hair with strings of jewels. She put on her shining armor and slung her bow and arrows across her shoulder. She belted her sword to her side. Fully armed, she strode to the edge of heaven and met her brother as he reached the top of the sky pillar.

"Dear sister, I mean no harm," Susanowo cajoled. "From the beginning, I never meant to hurt you. Our father was cruel, sending me to the land of the dead. I only wanted to say good-bye to you before I left."

"How can I know that what you're saying is true?" Amaterasu asked him.

"Let us create children together. If the children I create are male, then you will know that my intentions are good," Susanowo told her.

"Then give me your sword," said Amaterasu. He handed her his sword, and Amaterasu broke it into three parts. She crunched the parts in her teeth and blew the fragments away. From the mist of her breath were born three goddesses, lovelier than stars.

Susanowo took the jeweled necklace that Amaterasu wore and crunched the jewels in his teeth, then blew away the fragments. From the mist of his breath were born five gods, princes of heaven.

So Amaterasu saw that her brother's heart was pure. Susanowo left her and went willingly to the land of the dead, where he will remain for all eternity. And from that time forward, Amaterasu has ruled over heaven in peace and tranquillity.

INANNA, QUEEN OF HEAVEN AND EARTH

AN ANCIENT SUMERIAN GODDESS

The myth of Inanna may be more than four thousand years old. It comes from the ancient civilization of Sumer, situated in the valley between the Tigris and Euphrates rivers, in modern-day Iraq. This area is known as the cradle of civilization because it is the first place in the world where people practiced the art of agriculture and built great cities. The Sumerians worshiped Inanna, the goddess of the morning and evening star. Her special city was the city of Uruk, where a great temple was built in her honor. She was responsible for introducing agriculture to humankind, and she was also a goddess of fertility. The Sumerians wrote their myths on clay tablets, which were later found by archaeologists. Modern scholars have spent many years deciphering the tablets that tell the myths of Inanna.

In the first years, the very first years, when everything needed was brought into being, Inanna decided to go and visit her grandfather Enki, the god of wisdom. She set sail in the boat of heaven and sailed across the sea to Enki's palace.

Enki saw her coming, and he was pleased. How beautiful she was! When Inanna

arrived at the door to his palace, he greeted her respectfully. He offered her cakes and honey, and Inanna ate. He gave her beer to drink. Together Inanna and Enki drank many pitchers of beer, until they were drunk.

"Inanna, my most beautiful granddaughter, what shall I give you?" Enki asked her. "Inanna, I will give you my wisdom. I will give you power over the people of the earth. I will give you my crown of kingship!"

Inanna looked into her grandfather's eyes. "I accept!" she said.

"But, Inanna, I will give you more. I will give you power over all of heaven. I will give you the most sacred throne of the gods and the scepter of rulership!"

Inanna smiled. "I accept," she said.

"Dearest child, Inanna," Enki continued. "I will give you the art of planting and harvesting. I give you the art of the shepherd, the potter, the weaver. The lion and the leopard will come when you call them."

"I accept," said Inanna.

Then Enki, most powerful of the gods, fell into a deep and drunken sleep. Inanna loaded her gifts onto the boat of heaven. Swiftly she rowed back to her city, Uruk.

When Enki awoke, he looked about for his crown of kingship. He looked for the throne of the gods. He looked for the art of planting and harvesting, of shepherding and potting and weaving. But all his treasures were gone.

"Where is my sacred throne? Where is my crown? Where are my secret arts?" Enki asked his servant Isimud.

"My lord, you have given them to your granddaughter Inanna," Isimud answered.

"Go quickly and bring them back!" Enki cried in dismay.

Enki's servant Isimud found Inanna rowing the boat of heaven up the river Euphrates. "My master says you must return the gifts he has given you," he told her.

Inanna grew angry. "My grandfather lied to me! He said these gifts were mine, and now he wants to change his mind. Tell him I will not give them back," she answered, and kept on rowing.

Isimud returned to Enki's palace with Inanna's message. Now Enki sent an army of wild dragons to bring back his treasures by force.

Inanna saw the wild dragons flying toward her. She called to Ninshubar, her loyal servant. "Ninshubar, dearest friend, help me now. Save the boat of heaven and the treasures my grandfather Enki promised me."

Ninshubar stood on the wall of Inanna's sacred garden. She raised her arms in the air and screamed. Her scream sent the wild dragons hurtling back to their dens. Inanna rowed her boat safely into her city.

She gave her people the art of planting and harvesting, of shepherding and potting and weaving. She put the crown of kingship upon her head. She sat on the throne of the gods.

When Enki learned that Inanna had escaped his army of wild dragons, he gave her his blessing. "Inanna, you may keep the gifts I gave you," he told her. "Let them stay in your city. The people of Uruk will prosper. Your fields will be fertile; your animals will bear many young. May there always be friendship between earth and heaven."

The citizens of Uruk planted grain and harvested bushels of wheat and flax and barley. They wove fine linen clothes. They shaped beautiful pots and cups from clay. Dates and almonds and pistachio nuts grew in their orchards. Their sheep and goats gave birth to lambs and kids.

Inanna married the shepherd Dumuzi, and he became king. All of the city celebrated their marriage. Their gardens were overflowing with flowers. Goats produced more milk than the people could drink. The sheep gave birth to triplets. The pomegranate trees grew heavy with fruit as Inanna and Dumuzi walked together through their orchards.

Inanna gave birth to two sons, Shara and Lulal. They grew tall and strong.

The people of Inanna's city tilled their fields and tended their flocks. The fields of

Inanna's kingdom were thick with grain. The sheep and goats had plenty of green grass to eat. Their milk was sweet as honey. The lion and the leopard came out of the wild forests to sit by Inanna's side, and she gave them milk to drink. The rains came and watered the new seeds. The sun shone brightly and warmed the young seedlings.

But Inanna was not happy. She was restless. When she walked through her holy garden, she hardly noticed the flowers growing there. When the birds sang to greet the new day, she didn't hear them.

Inanna wanted to visit her sister, Ereshkigal, the queen of the dead. Inanna wanted to see the land of the dead from which no one returns. "My grandfather Enki went to the underworld," she said to herself, "and he returned. If my grandfather Enki can go, then so can I."

Ereshkigal's husband, Gugalanna, had died. Ereshkigal mourned for her husband. "I will go to comfort my sister," Inanna told her servant Ninshubar. "I will go to Gugalanna's funeral."

"No, Inanna, don't go," Ninshubar warned her mistress. "No one returns from the land of the dead. If you go, you will die as well."

"I will return," Inanna said. "I am queen of heaven and earth. I can go anywhere, even to the great below. But, Ninshubar, wait for me here. If three days pass and I have not returned, tell all the world to mourn for me. Go to the gods and beg them to rescue me."

Then Inanna prepared herself for the descent to the great below. She put the shining crown of heaven upon her head. She fastened a necklace of lapis beads around her neck. She slipped a golden bracelet on her wrist. She wrapped herself in her cloak of stars. She slipped on her silver shoes. She took her lapis measuring rod in her hand.

She journeyed to the outer walls of the underworld and knocked loudly upon the gate.

"Who is there?" the gatekeeper called out.

"It is I, Inanna, come to visit my sister, Ereshkigal. Let me pass."

"If you wish to enter the underworld, give up your crown," the gatekeeper commanded.

Inanna gave him her crown. She continued to the second gate.

"What do you want?" the second gatekeeper demanded.

"I want to see my sister, Ereshkigal, queen of the great below."

"Give me your shoes, and I will let you pass," the gatekeeper growled.

Inanna gave him her shoes. Barefoot and bareheaded, she went on to the third gate.

"Where are you going?" the keeper of the third gate asked her.

"I am going to comfort my sister, Ereshkigal, whose husband, Gugalanna, has died," Inanna answered.

"Give me your golden bracelet, and I will let you pass," hissed the gatekeeper.

Inanna gave him her bracelet. She continued on her way. She came to the fourth gate and knocked loudly.

"Why are you here?" the keeper of the fourth gate asked her.

"I am here to visit your queen, Ereshkigal the fair," Inanna replied.

"If you wish to enter the great below, give me your pretty necklace," the fourth gate-keeper insisted.

What could she do? Inanna gave him her necklace of lapis beads. She continued down to the great below.

The fifth gatekeeper asked for her measuring rod, and Inanna gave it to him. The sixth gatekeeper took her cloak of stars. Naked and cold, Inanna passed through the seventh gate. She entered the chamber of the mighty Ereshkigal.

Ereshkigal sat upon her throne. Around her neck she wore a necklace of human skulls. Upon her head she wore the crown of death. Her eyes were empty sockets, as black as onyx. She turned her empty eyes on Inanna. "Who are you?" she whispered. "Why have you come?"

"Ereshkigal!" Inanna cried. "It is your sister, Inanna! Don't you remember me? I've come to comfort you."

Inanna held out her empty hands and started toward her sister. Ereshkigal let out a howl of rage. She struck Inanna with cold, bony hands stronger than iron. She struck all the life out of her. Then she picked up her sister's corpse and hung it on a hook outside her door.

In the world above, three days had passed. Inanna did not return. Ninshubar began to beat the temple drums. "Inanna, your queen, is gone to the land of the dead," she proclaimed to the people. "Weep for your queen, who is lost in the great below. "

The citizens of Uruk wept for their queen.

Ninshubar ran swiftly to the island of the gods. "Inanna is gone," she told first one god and then another. "Inanna is lost in the great below."

When wise old Enki heard the news, he was deeply troubled. "What has my granddaughter done?" he cried. "How could Inanna, star of the evening, star of the morning, be lost in the great below? It cannot happen."

Enki scraped some dirt from under his fingernail. He rolled it into two small creatures, tiny as two houseflies. He breathed on the creatures with the breath of life. He gave them the food of life to eat and the water of life to drink. Then he told them, "Go to the underworld and bring my granddaughter Inanna back to us."

The two little creatures understood. They flew away to the underworld. They slipped through the cracks in the door and entered Ereshkigal's throne room.

Ereshkigal lay on the floor weeping and moaning. All the dead souls were eating up her insides. It hurt her.

"Oh, my belly!" she said with a sigh.

"Oh, your poor belly!" said the tiny creatures with a sigh.

"Oh, my head!" wailed Ereshkigal.

"Oh, your poor head!" wailed the tiny creatures.

"Oh, my heart!" moaned the queen of death.

"Oh, your poor heart!" moaned the tiny creatures.

Ereshkigal looked at the little creatures in amazement. "Who are you?" she asked them. "Who would come to this dark and lonely place to comfort me? I thank you for it. Let me give you a gift."

"Give us the corpse that hangs on a hook outside your door," cried the tiny creatures.

"Take it," Ereshkigal said.

The tiny creatures sprinkled Inanna with the water of life. They fed her the food of life. Inanna awoke. She began to climb from the underworld.

"Wait!" cried a terrible voice. Inanna stood frozen. She could not move. The demons of the underworld held her fast.

"No one leaves the underworld unmarked," they taunted her. "If you wish to leave here, you must send another in your place."

Inanna climbed up from the underworld, but the demons clung to her side. Inanna left the underworld and returned to her city of Uruk, surrounded by demons.

Just outside the palace gates Inanna found Ninshubar lying in the dust. She was weeping because she believed Inanna had died.

"Walk on, Inanna," said the demons. "We will take Ninshubar in your place."

"No!" she cried. "Not Ninshubar! Ninshubar is my dearest friend, my constant support, my wise adviser, and my warrior. When I did not return from the land of the dead, it was she who called upon the gods to rescue me. It was she who reminded my people to mourn for me. No, I will never give you Ninshubar."

"Walk on, Inanna," said the demons. "We will go with you to the palace."

Inside the palace gates Inanna found her son Shara lying in the dust, weeping for his mother because he believed she was dead. When Shara saw Inanna, he threw his arms about her knees.

"Walk on, Inanna," hissed the demons. "We will take Shara in your place."

"No!" cried Inanna. "Not Shara! He is my son who sings hymns to me, my comfort and my joy. I will never give you Shara."

"Very well, Inanna," whispered the demons. "Walk on, and we will come with you."

Inanna passed through the palace courtyard. There she saw her son Lulal, dressed in rags of mourning, with ashes on his face. He was weeping because he believed his mother was dead. When he saw Inanna, he threw himself at her feet.

"Walk on, Inanna," hissed the demons. "We will take Lulal in your place."

"No!" cried Inanna. "Not my son Lulal! Lulal is a leader among men. He is my right arm and my left arm. I will never let you take Lulal."

"Very well, Inanna. Walk on to your sacred garden. We will go with you."

Inanna walked through the palace and entered her sacred garden. There she saw her husband, Dumuzi, sitting on her throne of heaven. He was wearing his most splendid royal robes. He was playing a merry tune upon his reed pipe. Inanna saw that her husband, Dumuzi, did not weep for her. While she wandered alone in the land of the dead he had hardly noticed she was gone.

Inanna grew hot with anger. She looked on Dumuzi with the eye of death. "Take him!" she cried to the demons. "Take Dumuzi in my place!"

The demons broke Dumuzi's pipe into pieces. They seized him by the legs and threw him on the floor. They beat him and struck him with axes.

Dumuzi let out a wail. He called up to heaven to his brother-in-law Utu, god of justice and mercy. He begged Utu to help him escape the demons.

Utu, god of the sun, took pity on Dumuzi. Utu changed him into a snake. Now the demons could no longer hold him, and the snake slid away. Dumuzi ran from the demons, but they pursued him. He ran to his sister Geshtinanna's house, but the demons were close behind him. Dumuzi ran and hid himself in the home of his friend, but when the demons came looking for him, his friend was afraid and pointed out where Dumuzi was hiding.

The demons seized Dumuzi, but Utu changed him into a gazelle. In the shape of a gazelle, Dumuzi ran back to Geshtinanna's house. He hid with the sheep and the goats in her sheep pen. But the demons found him and seized him and held him fast. They dragged him away to the land of the dead.

The city of Uruk mourned for Dumuzi, the shepherd. The people of Uruk wept for their king. Inanna, no longer angry, wept for her husband. Geshtinanna wandered about the city looking for her lost brother.

"Oh, where is he, where is he?" she cried again and again. "Let me go with Dumuzi. Let me share my brother's fate."

Inanna was touched by Geshtinanna's grief. She took her hand and spoke to her gently. "Geshtinanna, I do not know where Dumuzi is. If I knew, I would send you to him. But he is gone. The demons have taken him, and I don't know where."

A little fly heard them talking and flew around their heads. "If I tell you where to find Dumuzi, what will you give me?" he asked Inanna.

"Oh, little fly, if you can help me find my husband, every kitchen in the world will be your home. I will let you live in the taverns and inns. I will let you rest in the company of the wise and powerful. When the finest musicians play, you will be there to hear their music," Inanna replied.

So the fly told them where to find Dumuzi, on the windswept plains in the kingdom of Ereshkigal. Inanna and Geshtinanna traveled there together. They found Dumuzi weeping, alone on the dark plains of the underworld.

Inanna took his hand. "Dumuzi," she said, "take heart. You will live in the underworld for half the year. When half the year has passed, your sister, since she wishes it, will take your place. When she is called below, you will return to me. When you are called, she will return."

So it has been throughout eternity. For half the year Dumuzi lives with Ereshkigal in the land of the dead. During this time the fields lie fallow and the flocks of sheep bear no young. But when Geshtinanna comes to take his place, Dumuzi returns to Inanna, the queen of heaven, and spring comes to the earth.

DURGA, THE WARRIOR GODDESS
A HINDU DEITY

The goddess Durga is one of the most popular of the Hindu deities. She is best known as a warrior goddess who protects the cosmos from evil demons. In times past, festivals were held in her honor to bring the Indian rulers success in battle. But she is also honored as an agricultural goddess who brings wealth and a bountiful harvest, and Durga is sometimes considered to be the earth itself, as well as the spirit that maintains cosmic harmony. In battle, Durga creates female deities out of herself, who help her slay demons. These goddesses are known as the Mothers. Kali, the most famous of these goddesses, is the important Hindu goddess of death and rebirth.

Once, in ages long past, a demon named Sumbha went to war with the gods. He took away the power of the sun and the moon and the stars, and threw the gods down from their heavenly kingdoms to wander on the earth like mortals. All of heaven and earth was thrown into chaos and darkness, and the conquered gods wandered helplessly on the earth.

One evening Sumbha saw Durga bathing in the waters of the Ganges River, and he was filled with desire for her. Sumbha had already taken for himself all the finest treasures of the universe. Now he decided that Durga's power, too, must belong to him. He sent his two faithful servants, Canda and Munda, to ask Durga to marry him.

Canda and Munda went straightaway to the goddess's dwelling, high in the shining Himalayas. "Oh, most beautiful one!" they greeted her. "We bring you a message from our lord, Sumbha, king of the demons. Sumbha, the commander of earth and heaven, conqueror of the gods, must always be obeyed. He has taken for himself all the treasures of the world. The sun and the moon are in his power. The elephants, bearers of the gods, are now for him alone. The jewels of the ocean are his. You, who are a jewel among women, should come with us and marry Sumbha. Then you will rule over the universe as his queen."

When Durga heard the demon's message, she smiled and spoke sweetly to his servants. "Everything you say is true," she said. "Unfortunately, long ago I foolishly promised that I would only marry a man whose strength was equal to my own. If Sumbha wishes to marry me, he must first conquer me on the battlefield."

When Sumbha received the goddess's reply, he laughed. Who was this woman to challenge him, king of the demons and lord of the universe? He commanded his chief general, Eyes of Smoke, to carry Durga back to him by force.

Eyes of Smoke surrounded Durga's mountain with his armies. "Follow me at once to the dwelling of your lord and master, Sumbha, king of the demons," the general bellowed at Durga. "If you do not come with me obediently, I will seize you and drag you there by your hair!"

"What can I do about it? Take me by force, then," said the goddess with a shrug.

Hearing this, Eyes of Smoke rushed forward to seize the mighty Durga. With a menacing *hum—hmmmmmmh!* the goddess reduced him to ashes. Then, she let loose a rain of arrows that fell on the cowering demon armies, and the demons scattered in terror. Finally, she sent her faithful lion out onto the battlefield, where he devoured as many demons as he could catch.

When Sumbha learned that Eyes of Smoke had been reduced to ashes and his armies wasted by the goddess's lion, he called once again for his servants Canda and

Munda. He ordered them to take the rest of his forces and capture the goddess, kill her lion, and deliver her to his palace in chains.

Canda and Munda gathered together a mighty host of evil beings, demons and goblins and ogres of every sort, and surrounded the Himalayas. On top of the highest golden mountain peak, they found the goddess Durga seated on her lion's back and smiling peacefully. The mighty demons got ready to seize her, circling with swords drawn and bows bent.

Durga gave a mighty war cry, and her face twisted into a hideous grin. From the top of her forehead there sprang a terrible creature carrying a sword and noose with one hand and a black, skull-topped staff with another. Around her neck she wore a necklace of human heads, and her dress was a tiger's skin. Her blue-black skin hung loosely on her emaciated form, while her three red eyes whirled with rage. This was Kali, the destroyer.

Licking her shriveled lips with her long, lolling tongue, Kali fell on the demon armies. She pulverized the cavalry with her teeth and swallowed the elephant riders in great, greedy gulps. She grabbed some of the demons in her arms and crushed them against her chest. Others she ground beneath her dancing feet. The arrows and stones that the demons hurled at her she caught in her mouth and crunched to bits. The mighty army of the demons was utterly destroyed. When Canda saw his army laid waste, he rushed at Kali and showered her with arrows. Munda threw a thousand discuses at her. But she opened her dreadful mouth and swallowed them all, like a black cloud swallowing a thousand suns. Then Kali laughed loudly, making a terrible cackling sound.

Now Durga leaped onto her lion's back and raced toward Canda. Seizing him by the hair, she cut off his head with her sword. When Munda saw the brave Canda fall, he rushed at Durga. Soon he, too, had fallen beneath the goddess's sword, and his severed head rolled across the battlefield.

Laughing loudly, Kali ran to retrieve the heads of Canda and Munda, and brought them to Durga. "Here is a present from me to you, my sister," she said with a smile. "Now you yourself can kill Sumbha."

"Thank you, dear Kali," said Durga playfully. "Since you have brought me Canda's and Munda's heads, from this day forth you will have a new nickname. We will call you the goddess Camunda because you are stronger than the strongest of the demons."

On learning of the deaths of Canda and Munda, Sumbha, the king of the demons, lost all his senses and became crazed with rage. He called on all the remaining demons to marshal their forces for a final onslaught on the goddess Durga. Then Sumbha himself went to meet the goddess, surrounded by thousands upon thousands of his magnificent troops.

From her place high on the mountaintop, Durga saw them coming, and she filled the sky with arrows shot from her bow. The earth rumbled with the mighty roars of her lion. Beside her stood Kali, her mouth hanging open, her snarls even louder than the lion's roar. When the demon troops heard this awful sound, they became frenzied and rushed at Durga from all four sides.

At this moment, in order to destroy the enemies of the gods and ensure the well-being of the divine powers, seven goddesses came to stand beside the mighty Durga.

Brahmani arrived in a chariot drawn by swans.

Mahesvari rode up on a giant bull, carrying a trident in each hand. She wore serpents on her arms for bracelets, and the crescent moon shone from her forehead.

Vaisnavi rode upon a stallion, with her arms full of weapons.

Kaumari came in the form of a sow.

Narasimhi came in the form of a lion, and each time she shook her mane, the sky was scattered with stars.

Then Aindri, who has a thousand eyes, appeared mounted on the lord of elephants. She carried a thunderbolt in her hand.

Finally, a terrible spirit sprang from the body of Durga herself, gruesome and yapping like a thousand jackals.

Seeing the seven goddesses, they who are called the Mothers, the arrogant demons unloosed a rain of arrows, lances, and spears. Durga playfully broke all the weapons that were tossed at her. Meanwhile, Kali roamed the battlefield, ripping open demons with her sword and crushing others with her skull-topped staff. And all the Mothers fell on Sumbha's warriors and killed them by the thousands, until those who remained scattered like ashes in the wind.

Then the great, cruel Raktabija, mightiest of the demon warriors, strode into the battle. Aindri struck him with one of her thunderbolts, and blood gushed from his chest. But as soon as the blood had touched the ground, it shaped itself into the form of another soldier as mighty as Raktabija himself. Vaisnavi wounded him with her discus and Kaumari with her spear. But each drop of blood that fell from Raktabija's body was immediately transformed into another demon just like him, so that soon the world was once more filled with fierce, fighting demons. And these men born of blood fell on the Mothers with their terrible weapons and began to beat them back. Blood fell in torrents to the earth, and the gods were utterly terrified.

Now Durga, seeing the destruction that Raktabija had wrought, called on Kali to save them all. "Oh, Camunda," she said to the death goddess, "open wide your mouth. Drink up the blood that falls from this demon warrior before it reaches the ground. Devour all the demons who are born from him. Go quickly, or all is lost!"

With a triumphant laugh the ever-hungry Kali ran out onto the battlefield followed by Durga, who struck Raktabija with her spear. Soon the mighty Raktabija lay dead on the battlefield, all of his blood drained from him. Then Kali fell on him and began to drink his blood. She drank every last drop of it. She also took the demons born from his blood directly into her mouth, chewed them up, and devoured them. The goddesses then danced around Raktabija's body joyfully.

Now that his mightiest warrior had fallen, now that all his armies had been wasted, Sumbha himself rode out onto the battlefield. All he could think of was to kill this dreadful goddess and have his revenge. In a blind rage, Sumbha rushed forward in his chariot. Durga saw him coming and rang her bell, filling the four directions with its sound. Her lion roared, and Kali pounded the earth with her hands, making a fearful drumming noise. "Stop! Stop, you wicked one!" Durga cried.

"Why should I stop?" demanded Sumbha. "Oh, Durga, you are puffed up with pride, but you have no true strength to fight me. You rely on others to do your fighting for you. If you and I were to meet one-on-one, like true warriors, I could easily beat you."

"Do you think so, Sumbha?" said Durga with a laugh. "But who are these others you speak of? I alone exist in this world. No one is second to me. Watch, oh wicked one, while these manifestations of my power return to me."

Then Durga held out her arms, and all the goddesses disappeared inside of her, until there was only she, alone. "Through my extraordinary power I can appear in many forms. Now I stand as I truly am, utterly alone. May you be resolute in combat," said Durga.

With these words she struck at Sumbha with her spear. She pierced him with her arrows and crushed him with her club. Whatever weapon the demon king attacked her with, she broke with her bare hands, as if it were a child's toy. When all his weapons were broken, Sumbha rushed at her and struck her with his fist, but she easily wrestled him to the ground and struck him so hard that he was forced to turn and run from her. He ran up to the sky, but she chased after him until she caught him and threw him back down to earth. Then the goddess broke open his chest with her spear, and all the life breath went out of him and he was utterly broken.

As soon as the demon king died, the sun and moon returned to their place in the sky. The waters of the world began to flow again, as they should. When the wicked one was dead, the whole universe grew calm. The winds blew favorably, sacred fires burned peacefully, and the gods returned joyfully to their kingdom in the heavens. And so it has been from that day to this, thanks to the mighty Durga.

MAWU, THE CREATOR

SUPREME BEING TO THE FON PEOPLE

Among the Fon people of Dahomey, West Africa, the supreme being is called Mawu-Lisa, or sometimes simply Mawu. The creator of all, Mawu-Lisa is neither male nor female. When the Dahomeans speak of Mawu-Lisa, they say that Mawu is the female side of god and Lisa is the male side of god. This myth of Mawu explains how death and magic came into the world.

In the beginning of everything, there was Mawu-Lisa, who has two faces. The first face is that of a woman whose name is Mawu, and her eyes are the moon. The second face is that of a man whose name is Lisa, and his eyes are the sun.

Mawu gave birth to all of the gods. Her youngest child is Legba. Because he is the youngest, Legba is spoiled. He has no home of his own and lives with his mother. He is the only one of Mawu's children who knows all her different languages. Mawu taught each of the gods a different language so that none of them could understand everything that happens and become too powerful. If one god wishes to speak to another, he must send his message through Legba.

Because Legba is Mawu's favorite, she made him more powerful than all the rest of

the gods. She gave him magic. And since Legba loved to play tricks, he decided to use his magic to have some fun.

One day he came down to the world and, using magic, turned a vine into a poisonous snake. Then he put the snake on the road. Soon a woman walked by on her way to the market, and Legba commanded the snake to bite her. After the snake bit the woman, Legba said, "If you give me two chickens and a calabash of palm wine, I will give you a magic charm to make you well."

The woman got sick from the snakebite. She feared she might die. She gave Legba the two chickens and the calabash of wine, and he gave her a magic charm to make her well. After that he told the snake to bite another person and made that person pay for a charm to get well. He played this trick again and again, and in this way he soon became rich.

One day a clever and curious man named Awe came by and watched what Legba was doing. "What is that thing that bites people?" he asked, pointing at the snake.

"That is magic," Legba told him. "If you bring me a goat and eighty cowries and some straw, I will make one for you, too."

Awe brought Legba what he asked for, and Legba taught Awe how to make a snake from a vine, the kind that bites people and makes them sick. Then Legba gave him a charm to cure the sickness. Soon the charms spread everywhere. If someone had a problem, he would go to Awe and pay him for a charm to cure it. Awe would give some of the money to Legba, and Legba would teach him how to make a charm to cure that person's problem.

Up in the sky world, Mawu soon heard what Legba and Awe were doing on earth. She became angry. She knew it was a bad idea to have magic in the world. As punishment, she made Legba into an invisible spirit so that he could no longer live among people. But Awe was a man, and Awe continued to make magic. He became the greatest magician in the world. He gave charms to anyone who could pay him for them. Some of the charms helped people, but he also gave charms to those who wished to do evil.

The kings of many lands came to Awe and asked for his charms. In this way Awe became more powerful than anyone on earth. He was even more powerful than the kings, for he could always use his magic to take away the kings' power. Everyone was afraid of him.

At last Awe decided that he had learned everything there was to know in this world. He was so powerful, he thought he must be more powerful than Mawu herself. He decided to go up to the sky and test his strength against the creator.

First, he bought some cotton thread, and all night long he rolled the thread into a ball, from dusk until dawn. Then, he bought some silk thread, and all day long he rolled it into a ball, from dawn until dusk. When the cotton thread and the silk thread both measured the same length, he climbed an anthill and threw his balls of thread into the sky. Mawu caught them and held on tight. Then, Awe climbed the threads up to the sky.

When Awe arrived before the creator, he told her, "My knowledge is great. I wish to measure my knowledge with Mawu."

Mawu smiled at him. "Show me, then. I have given life to the people on earth. Why don't you make a living person, too?"

Awe cut down a tree and began to carve a human figure. He carved it very carefully, until it looked exactly like a human being. But the figure could not talk. It couldn't breathe or laugh or move. It was just a wooden statue. Awe breathed on the statue. He chanted magic spells and rubbed magic ointment on the statue. But no matter what he did, the statue was still a statue. He couldn't bring the statue to life.

At last Mawu stopped him. "Foolish Awe," she said with a laugh. "Do you really think you are more powerful than Mawu, the mother of all? I alone know how to give life. No one else can ever understand this magic, and no one else will ever be as powerful as I."

Then Mawu opened her hand, and in it was a grain of corn. She placed the corn on the ground and covered it with soil. Within moments the little seed had sprouted into a full-grown plant, weighed down by many ears of corn. Mawu harvested the corn and ground the grain into flour. With the flour she prepared dinner for Awe.

After Awe had eaten his fill, Mawu sent him back to earth. But she worried about the trouble he might cause there, and sent Death to follow him.

Awe saw Death creeping up behind him. He used one of his magic charms to capture Death and bind him fast.

From her home up in the sky, Mawu saw what had happened. Awe could never know how to create life, but he had become clever enough to conquer Death.

"Awe, listen to me!" Mawu called down to the magician. "If you, Awe, attack Death, I will take away fire from humankind. No one will be able to cook food, and you will all go hungry. Everyone will be cold at night. There will be nothing to guard you from wild animals. Think about it, Awe."

Awe thought carefully about Mawu's words. He realized that if she took away fire, all of humankind would suffer. Everyone on earth would be cold and hungry. So he gave Death back to Mawu. Now when people are hungry, they can cook food and eat. When they are cold, they can warm themselves. When wild animals threaten them, they can scare them away with fire.

Mawu was satisfied. "You've done well, Awe. You may keep your magic, but remember to use it for good and not for evil. If someone is ill, you must take good care of him. But if I choose, I will send Death to kill him. Don't try to stop me, for that is how things must be."

And that is how things are, from that day to this.

AFTERWORD

A long time ago there were Goddesses everywhere. They lived among us and helped us to find food and find a warm place to live and be close to our families. They taught the people of the earth to live in balance with nature and in harmony with one another. They were so powerful that no dark spirits could come close to the people of the earth and frighten them with thoughts of war and terror and bloodshed.

Then something changed. I don't know what happened, but the Goddesses were forgotten by the people of the earth. They didn't disappear altogether, but they stepped back from so many people's lives. A new feeling came to this planet. People turned away from their Goddesses and began to embrace the Gods of War and Terror and Vengeance. We forgot the wisdom the Goddesses had shared with us so freely.

We forgot the message of Changing Woman, who taught us that all must live together in peace and harmony.

We forgot the message of Macha, who reminds us that all women are free.

We forgot the message of Sedna, who taught us to tend our oceans and treasure the creatures of the sea.

We forgot the message of Kuan Yin, who told us that all are deserving of compassion.

We could no longer hear the words of Isis, who reminds us to gather together the fragments of our lives when our lives have been shattered, so that from the broken pieces we can make something whole and beautiful.

We forgot to honor Ix Chel, the Goddess of the Moon, who teaches us the meaning of what is empty and what is full.

We forgot about Amaterasu, the Sun Goddess, who warms us each day with her radiance.

We forgot the message of Inanna, who told us that from the darkness light will come.

We forgot the power of Durga, who can help us chase away the demons and restore order to the universe.

We forgot the message of Mawu-Lisa, the Creator, who taught us that all must live with respect for the power of she who brings life and she who blesses us with death when our bodies have grown too tired to do the work that needs to be done.

* * *

The people of this earth forgot about the Goddesses for so many thousands of years that it was almost as if the Goddesses had never lived among us. It was almost as if the time of the Goddesses was only a dream, the kind of dream that you forget as soon as you open your eyes in the morning.

But now something is changing again. Now the people of the earth are starting to remember. We remember that the Goddesses are alive and they are waiting to answer our prayers. They want us to remember them so that they can help us heal all the pain and suffering that exists on this beautiful planet. They want us to give up our dreams of war and vengeance and bloodshed and remember that we are a people who were born to love one another and celebrate the beauty of the earth with every breath we take.

—Katrin Hyman Tchana

SOURCES

General Sources:

Baring, Anne, and Jules Cashford. *The Myth of the Goddess: Evolution of an Image*. New York: Viking Press, 1991.

Kinsley, David. *The Goddesses' Mirror: Visions of the Divine from East and West*. Albany, N.Y.: State University of New York Press, 1989.

Larrington, Carolyne, ed. *The Feminist Companion to Mythology*. London: Pandora Press, 1992.

Olson, Carl, ed. *The Book of the Goddess, Past and Present: An Introduction to Her Religion*. New York: Crossroad Publishing Co., 1983.

Stone, Merlin. *Ancient Mirrors of Womanhood: A Treasury of Goddess and Heroine Lore from Around the World*. Boston: Beacon Press, 1984.

Changing Woman:

Haile, Father Berard. *Origin Legend of the Navaho Enemy Way*. Yale University Publications in Anthropology, no. 17. New Haven, Conn.: Yale University Press, 1938.

Haile, Father Berard. *The Upward Moving and Emergence Way: The Gishin Biye' Version*. Lincoln: University of Nebraska Press, 1981.

Klah, Hasteen. *Navajo Creation Myth: The Story of the Emergence*. Santa Fe, N. Mex.: Museum of Navajo Ceremonial Art, 1942.

Matthews, Washington, comp. and trans. *Navaho Legends*. Salt Lake City: University of Utah Press, 1994.

Moon, Sheila. *Changing Woman and Her Sisters: Feminine Aspects of Selves and Deities*. San Francisco: Guild for Psychological Studies Publishing House, 1984.

Wyman, Leland C. *Blessingway*. Tucson: University of Arizona Press, 1970.

Macha:

Cross, Tom Peete and Clark Harris Slover, eds. *Ancient Irish Tales*. New York: Henry Holt and Company, 1936.

Green, Miranda Jane. *Celtic Myths*. London: British Museum Press, 1993.

Green, Miranda. *The Gods of the Celts*. Gloucestershire, UK: Sutton Publishing, 1986.

Hull, Eleanor, comp. and ed. *The Cuchullin Saga in Irish Literature: Being a Collection of Stories Relating to the Hero Cuchullin*. London: David Nutt, 1898.

MacCulloch, J. A. *The Religion of the Ancient Celts*. London: Constable, 1991. First published 1911 by T&T Clark.

Sedna:

Boas, Franz. *The Central Eskimo*. Lincoln: University of Nebraska Press, 1964.

Holtved, Erik. "The Eskimo Myth about the Sea-Woman." *Folk* 8–9 (1966–67): 145–153.

Millman, Lawrence. *A Kayak Full of Ghosts: Eskimo Tales*. Santa Barbara, Calif.: Capra Press, 1987.

Savard, Remi. "La Deese Sous-Marine des Eskimo." In *Echanges et Communications*, edited by Jean Poillon and Pierre Maranda. Paris: Mouton and Co., 1970.

Kuan Yin:

Johnson, Samuel. *Oriental Religions and Their Relation to Universal Religion*. Boston: Houghton, Osgood and Company, 1878.

Lim, Sian-tek. *Folk Tales from China*. New York: John Day Company, 1944.

Werner, E. T. C. *Myths and Legends of China*. London: Harrap, 1922.

Isis:

Baring, Anne and Jules Cashford. *The Myth of the Goddess: Evolution of an Image*. New York: Viking Press, 1991.

Bleeker, C. J. "Isis and Hathor: Two Ancient Egyptian Goddesses." In *The Book of the Goddesses, Past and Present: An Introduction to Her Religion*, edited by Carl Olson, 29–48. New York: Crossroad Publishing Company, 1987.

Brandon, S. G., ed. "Isis as Savior God." In *The Savior God*, edited by C. J. Bleeker, 1–16. Manchester, UK: Manchester University Press, 1963.

Egan, Rory B. "Isis: Goddess of the Oikoumene." In *Goddesses in Religion and Modern Debate*, edited by Larry W. Hurtado, 123–142. Atlanta: Scholars Press, 1990.

Kinsley, David. *The Goddesses' Mirror: Visions of the Divine from East and West*. Albany: State University of New York Press, 1989.

Plutarch. *Plutarch's Morals*. Translated by C. W. King. London: George Bell and Sons, 1882.

Wolkstein, Diane. *The First Love Stories: From Isis and Osiris to Tristan and Iseult*. New York: HarperCollins, 1991.

Ix Chel:

Ardren, Traci, ed. *Ancient Maya Women*. Walnut Creek, Calif.: AltaMira Press, 2002.

Bierhorst, John. *The Mythology of Mexico and Central America*. New York: William Morrow and Company, 1990.

Stone, Merlin. *Ancient Mirrors of Womanhood: A Treasury of Goddess and Heroine Lore from Around the World*. Boston: Beacon Press, 1984.

Thompson, J. Eric S. *Maya History & Religion*. Norman: University of Oklahoma Press, 1970.

Amaterasu:

Herbert, Jean. *Shintô: At the Fountain-head of Japan*. New York: Stein and Day Publishers, 1967.

MacKenzie, Donald A. *Myths of China and Japan*. London: Gresham Publishing, 1923.

Wheeler, Post. *The Sacred Scriptures of the Japanese*. New York: Henry Schuman, 1952.

Inanna:

Wolkstein, Diane and Samuel Noah Kramer. *Inanna, Queen of Heaven and Earth: Her Stories and Hymns from Sumer*. New York: Harper & Row, 1983.

Durga:

Coburn, Thomas B., trans. *Encountering the Goddess: A Translation of the Devî-Mâhâtmya and a Study of Its Interpretation*. Albany: State University of New York Press, 1991.

Kinsley, David R. *The Sword and the Flute: Kali and Krsna, Dark Visions of the Terrible and the Sublime in Hindu Mythology*. Berkeley: University of California Press, 1975.

Mawu:

Herskovits, Melville J., and Frances S. *Dahomean Narrative: A Cross Cultural Analysis*. Evanston, Ill.: Northwestern University Press, 1958.

Parrinder, Geoffrey. *African Mythology*. London: Paul Hamlyn, 1967.

Teish, Luisah. *Jambalaya: The Natural Woman's Book of Personal Charms and Practical Rituals*. San Francisco: Harper & Row, 1985.

AUTHOR'S NOTE

My father is Jewish, and my mother grew up going to the Lutheran church. The story in my family is that when they decided to get married, both the Jewish rabbi and the Lutheran pastor refused to perform the marriage ceremony. They said the union of two people from different faiths would be a sin. In fact, the story goes, the rabbi told my parents that any child they had would be "an abomination." My parents got married anyway, in a civil ceremony performed in the nondenominational chapel at my father's college. A few years later the "abomination" who wrote this book was born.

One result of my parents' foiled attempts to marry in a religious ceremony was that I grew up without any formal religious education. Nonetheless, I thought long and hard about God the creator and yearned to be closer to him. In first grade I drew a picture of God. I knew exactly what he looked like: an old white man with a long, flowing beard who was somewhat ferocious but had a kindly side to him. I spent many hours worrying about how to stay on God's good side. My great-aunt Pat gave me a book of psalms, which I loved because it had a real silver binding inlaid with mother-of-pearl. I slept with that book under my pillow and read the psalms aloud to myself every day. I tried very hard to be good so that God would be pleased with me and grant all my wishes.

Where does this vision of God as an old man in the sky come from? I don't know, but the little half-Jewish girl growing up in Lyme, New Hampshire, in the 1960s never questioned that this was the real God, though she never went to church and doesn't remember ever talking about God with anyone. And when I ask my own African American sons, "What does God look like?" they tell me this: He is old. He is white. He has a long beard. He lives in the sky. Sometimes he is angry, but sometimes he is nice.

This image of our creator stopped working for me a long time ago. It didn't make me want to be good anymore. It didn't help me make difficult decisions. It didn't comfort me when I was sad. It didn't bring me closer to the wonderful mystery of existence. At some point I consciously decided to try to reenvision God as a female—not because I think the creator is a person, but because I need to be able to imagine the creator as a force that encompasses me and has meaning for me. And I am a woman.

So I practice calling God "she" and "her." Whenever I do this, my sons cry in aggravation, "Mommy! God is not a girl!" Oh, my darlings! It's not that I think God is a girl. God is everything, but God is a girl, too. At least that is my belief. I need to remember that God can also look something like me. Or something like my sons. Something like all of us.

I started to write this book when my mother and I were asked to collaborate on a collection of creation myths for young people. I began my research with long hours in the religion and mythology section of Dartmouth College Library, browsing through the mythological literature of many different cultures. One day I picked up a book called *When God Was a Woman*, by Merlin Stone. I was fascinated by Stone's hypotheses about an ancient matriarchal culture characterized by its reverence for a great mother goddess. I began to think about the mythological material I was reading in a new way. I wondered how the myths had changed over the millennia, and whether or not they preserved in them any glimmers of a forgotten culture, a culture in which goddesses were as powerful and as important as gods. I started to read more about goddesses. It was difficult to stay focused on my original search for creation myths.

I read about Epona, the horse goddess of the ancient Celts, and suddenly my early devotion to horses—one that is shared by so many young girls—took on new meaning. And I read the myth of Inanna, included in this collection, whose story of descent into death and subsequent rebirth seems to me symbolic of every woman's journey to maturity. The stories were beautiful, exciting, evocative. They resonated in me as powerfully as the Judeo-Christian stories I had grown up with. Why hadn't I read them before? I imagined how these myths might have helped me make sense of my life if only I had read them as a child. I knew that this was the book I needed to write: a collection of goddess myths for young people.

Thousands of goddesses have been worshiped around the world, both in ancient times and today. It would be impossible to include all their stories in one book, or even in a series of books. There are many goddesses from ancient cultures that very little is known about. We know of their existence only through the findings of archaeologists or as passing references in fragments of old manuscripts.

Other storytellers have chosen to invent goddess myths, taking what little is known about a goddess and creating their own story using her name. But for this collection I wanted to include only "authentic" myths—stories that evolved organically from the needs of ancient peoples and survived through the millennia. I have retold all the myths in this collection in order to make them appropriate for and accessible to young people today, and in the process may also have added details to flesh them out or make them read more smoothly. But the bones of these tales are not something I could possibly have made up. They come to us from the ancient ones.

In selecting the stories for this collection, I tried to choose goddesses from different cultures. My mother and I were committed to making books that reflect the wonderful diversity found in this country of ours, and we hope that in this book all children will find a small piece of their heritage.

But my criteria for selecting a myth were first and foremost those of a storyteller's. Is this a good story? Is it interesting? Is it exciting? Will children want to hear it again? To my regret, none of the Norse goddesses are represented here, because I couldn't find a myth that I knew how to retell in an interesting, exciting way. (This doesn't mean that such a myth doesn't exist—it just means I couldn't find it.) I also chose not to include any of the myths about the classical Greek goddesses. These myths are relatively well known, and there are already many retellings available. The myths in this collection are less familiar but equally compelling. They deserve to be told again and again.

Collecting these stories was a transformative experience for me. It gave me images of a creator that I carry with me always. In the years since I discovered them, the goddesses in this book have offered me strength when I feel overwhelmed, comfort when I am in distress, and clear vision when I am confused. If you ask, they will do the same for you.

ARTIST'S NOTE

When I began to work on this book, I was worried about doing the picture research for all of the goddesses. While there is quite a lot of material, visual and otherwise, from all of the cultures that these goddesses are from, there are no images whatsoever of most of them or the worlds they created. Still, in some innate way each of these stories felt very familiar to me. So when my daughter, Katrin, suggested that I contact the spirit of each goddess personally and ask how she would like to be portrayed in my pictures, I took her advice. I sat quietly in my studio with the goddesses and their stories as I waited for them to visit me and give me instructions. One by one, they appeared to me and shared their hearts and their souls, and I hope I've honored them all in the best way I could.

The goddesses also inspired me to try a new technique to create their portraits, so for the first time, I've used collage. For this I mixed handmade paper, odd bits of fabric, fleece from my own sheep, seeds from my own garden, and whatever odd things I found around the house; then I combined them with glue, inks, and acrylic paints.

Jacket: The goddess on the jacket is from a story I made up and drew when I was twelve years old. I painted her again when I was twenty-one, and then did a large oil painting of her when

I was forty. It was always the same, with interesting variations: a woman sleeping in an egg filled with light, summer, and life. The egg has landed in a cold, hostile, and dark winter forest. The people who live there have come to witness the miracle of sweetness, warmth, and light. They are frightened and curious. What should they do? If they leave the egg alone, will it eventually freeze? If they break the egg to set her free, will she die of the cold, or will the warmth, sweetness, and light escape? And if it does, will they die? What a dilemma, and what a strange story for a twelve-year-old to invent. When I had finished the pictures for the stories in this book, I thought of "my goddess" and painted her again for the cover. This time it was a collage version, but only for the landscape inside the egg. Two weeks after I finished the cover painting, I was searching in *The Encyclopedia of Myth and Legend* for something else, and I saw that my goddess had existed for centuries! She was real, and she was in my dreams through the collective unconscious and DNA. Her name is Ostara, and she was worshiped by ancient Germanic tribes. (My ancestry is German!) She's the goddess of light, spring, and rebirth. It is from *Ostara* that we get our word *Easter*.

Frontispiece: The goddess on the frontispiece is simply The Mother, who is the source of all goddess stories.

Underneath the face of *Changing Woman* are three carefully painted faces: a baby, a grown-up woman, and a very old woman. The face you see is the teenage face of White-Shell Woman, because this is still an important image for young Navajo women. The sun in this picture is made from a bit of fleece clipped from one of my sheep. This is because Changing Woman reminded me that the Navajo people have always been shepherds.

Macha is living every young girl's dream—to run with horses! The horses she is running with are dream horses and "real" horses. The black-and-white photographs of real horses were taken at dawn by my partner, Jean, who is also a horsewoman. Macha's undershirt is handmade paper. She would have taken off her surcoat in order to run. I love the feeling of speed and motion that the collaged horses give this picture.

Sedna sent me searching through all the natural history books for the marine life of northern Pacific waters—plus all the fascinating life that lives at the bottom of the sea.

Kuan Yin is one of the two goddesses in this book for whom I could find an existing image. In this case it was a third-century BCE statue of the goddess. I copied her robes, her sash, and her jade necklace from this stone goddess. I decided on a lotus for her crown and a peony for her pedestal only because it seemed to suit her. The edge of her green robe is taken from an ancient Chinese silk tapestry.

The suffering, anguished people are courtesy of the German artist Käthe Kollwitz, who understood human suffering more than any artist aside from Goya. The lame, insane, and blind beggars are from the paintings of Pieter Breughel the Elder, and the amazingly Chinese-looking landscape is also from one of Breughel's paintings.

Isis is set in a landscape that is a 1940s photo of Egyptian grain fields. The *River Nile* is a piece of brilliant sponge work from the kindergarten students of Open Fields School. The blood-soaked earth that Isis walks on is made of handmade paper. Her dress is made from torn tracing paper, and her headdress is hawk wings.

Ix Chel is riding in the moon, shining above the ruins of Machu Picchu, an ancient Mayan temple. The fabric she is weaving from her rainbow yarn is actually part of an antique herb bag from Peru.

Her hairstyle, earrings, loom, and simple white dress are all taken from ancient Mayan friezes. I used cheesecloth and nylon net to make her dress. Her friend, the evening star, is keeping her company.

Amaterasu's armor is made entirely of origami paper. Her bow and arrows, her sword, and her headdress are all from ancient Japanese paintings. The cloud she stands on is toilet paper, Kleenex, and tracing paper. Her brother's robes are also origami paper.

Inanna is the goddess of life and fertility. It was fun to find images of gardens, growth, and life. I used seed catalogs and cut-up photos from my own garden, a friend's garden, and Sissinghurst, Vita Sackville-West's garden. I dressed Inanna in her cloak of the stars and her crown of heaven. I gave her bracelets and her lapis measuring rod—and a bird that is indigenous to the region in the story. The seven gates that Innana had to pass through to visit her sister, Ereshkigal, the goddess of death, are symbolized by the odd rainbow that goes through Inanna's cloak. I think Ereshkigal speaks for herself.

Durga and *Kali* are my favorite goddesses in this collection because they are so strong and assertive! Durga is one of the goddesses who is pictured in ancient Hindu texts. Kali is also, but she takes on so many forms that it was difficult for me to settle on one. So I asked Durga, and she assured me that her sister/daughter was very like the vindictive and frightening image that I've invented, at least in this battle. Her necklace of skulls is made of tiny photocopies of children I know. Her noose is a real one made of twine. Durga is riding a lion that is a composite/collage of many lion pictures and my own painting. Her skirt is handmade paper and hippie ribbon. Her belt and bodice are from William Morris Wallpaper Reproductions. Her sword, battle-ax, bow and arrow, spear, and chakra (a razor-sharp ring that is twirled and released—fast!) are all in the old pictures of Durga. (Often she has twelve arms, but I couldn't handle all those weapons!)

It was *Mawu-Lisa* who told me to put the photographs of African people, the thorn tree, and the West African blue butterfly in her portrait. She also told me to use powerful tribal cicatrices (scars) to define her body and to make snake horns growing from her head to symbolize the duality of her gender.

My original painting was truer to the culture of this particular goddess. Appropriately, Mawu, the Creator, was portrayed in a more anatomically correct way than she is now. But since we didn't want to offend those who object to nudity in a children's book, changes were made. For this I apologize to my older readers, and to Mawu.